Art Lab for Little Kids

Art Lab for Little Kids

52 Playful Projects for Preschoolers!

Susan Schwake

Photography by Rainer Schwake

QUARRY

Quarto is the authority on a wide range of topics.

Quarto educates, entertains and enriches the lives of our readers—enthusiasts and lovers of hands-on living. www.QuartoKnows.com

First published in the United States of America in 2013 by
Quarry Books, an imprint of
Quarto Publishing Group USA Inc.
100 Cummings Center
Suite 406-L
Beverly, Massachusetts 01915-6101
Telephone: (978) 282-9590
Fax: (978) 283-2742
QuartoKnows.com
Visit our blogs at QuartoKnows.com

10 9 8 7 6 5

ISBN: 978-1-59253-836-2

Digital edition published in 2013
eISBN: 978-1-61058-766-2

Library of Congress Cataloging-in-Publication Data
Schwake, Susan.
  Art lab for little kids : 52 playful projects for preschoolers! / Susan Schwake.
     pages cm
  Summary: "Developed for the younger set (3–6 year olds) and targeting one of the most critical developmental periods for children, Art Lab for Little Kids is the perfect book for both parents and teachers who are seeking enriching and unique experiences to offer this age group. As in Susan Schwake's first book, *Art Lab for Kids* (Quarry Books, 2012), the Labs can be used as singular projects, or used to build up to a year of hands-on fine art experiences."— Provided by publisher.
  ISBN 978-1-59253-836-2 (pbk.)
  1. Art—Technique—Juvenile literature. I. Title.
  N7440.S393 2013
  372.5'044--dc23
                                                            2012045843

Book Layout: *tabula rasa* graphic design, www.trgraphicdesign.com
Series Design: John Hall Design Group, www.johnhalldesign.com
All photography by Rainer Schwake unless otherwise noted.
Developmental Editor: Marla Stefanelli

Printed in China

Dedication

This book is dedicated with love to my own (not so) littles,
Grace and Chloe, who have been the most creative and
loving daughters I could have ever dreamed of.

Contents

Introduction **8**

UNIT 1

Setting the Stage for Making Art 10
The Master Materials List **12**
Basic Methods for Handling Materials
  in the Studio **17**

UNIT 2

Drawing 26
Lab 1: Buttermilk Chalk **28**
Lab 2: Crayon Fun **30**
Lab 3: Dot to Dot **32**
Lab 4: Oil Pastels **34**
Lab 5: Ice Drawings **36**
Lab 6: Ink Spots **38**
Lab 7: Ink & Cotton Swabs **40**
Lab 8: Drawings on Fabric **42**
Lab 9: Marble Drawing **44**
Lab 10: Tape Flags **46**

UNIT 3

Painting 48
Lab 11: Spray-Bottle Paintings **50**
Lab 12: Pick a Brush **52**
Lab 13: Watercolor Magic **54**
Lab 14: Drip, Drop, Splat! **56**
Lab 15: Mixing It Up **58**
Lab 16: Cotton Ball Color **60**
Lab 17: That's Not a Brush! **62**
Lab 18: Where We Live **64**
Lab 19: Sweet Paintings **66**
Lab 20: Op Art **68**
Lab 21: Circle Paintings **70**

UNIT 4

Printmaking 72
Lab 22: Letter Prints **74**
Lab 23: Fold Me a Print **76**
Lab 24: Spuds! **78**
Lab 25: What's the Rub? **80**
Lab 26: Watercolor Monotypes **82**
Lab 27: Glue Prints **84**
Lab 28: Lace Prints **86**
Lab 29: Balloon Prints **88**
Lab 30: Let's Print Circles & Lines **90**

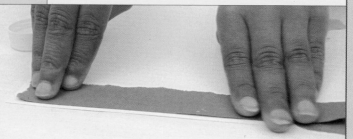

UNIT 5

Sculpture 92

Lab 31: Tinfoil Fun **94**
Lab 32: Mat Board Stacks **96**
Lab 33: Clay Play **98**
Lab 34: Tube Construction **100**
Lab 35: Masks **102**
Lab 36: Paper Vases **104**
Lab 37: Royal Crowns **106**
Lab 38: Mat Board Mobiles **108**
Lab 39: Fairy & Toad Houses **110**
Lab 40: Personal Piñatas **112**
Lab 41: Paper Mâché Minis **114**

UNIT 6

Mixed Media 116

Lab 42: Fabric Collage **118**
Lab 43: Sewing Cards **120**
Lab 44: Torn Paper Collage **122**
Lab 45: Wild Weavings **124**
Lab 46: Black & White & Red **126**
Lab 47: Wonderful Wallpaper **128**
Lab 48: Oil Pastels & Magazines **130**
Lab 49: Junk Drawer Collage **132**
Lab 50: Branch Weavings **134**
Lab 51: Sand & Glue Paintings **136**
Lab 52: Tape Shakers **138**

Resources for Materials **140**
Contributing Artists **141**
Acknowledgments **143**
Photo Credits **143**
About the Author **144**

Introduction

THIS BOOK IS A COLLECTION OF LESSONS for the littles in your life—the ones not quite tall enough to sit at "the big table." They are the ones who—if you listen carefully and provide them with opportunity—will surprise you most with their curiosity, creativity, and ability. I have had the pleasure of making art with people of all ages for the past twenty years in a wide variety of settings. Each time I work with a mixed-age group, I can't help but notice how the littler children are always the first to engage deeply and with pleasure right from the start. Sometimes by action and sometimes by observation—but always engaged. I believe that we are born creative; to nurture this quality from an early age is so very important! It is the creative minds among us that help us conquer the biggest challenges in our lives. It is my sincere hope that this book will inspire you to playfully engage yourself with a child to make art and nurture that creative seed.

Setting the Stage for Making Art

THIS UNIT WILL PREPARE YOU to make art with children and keep things comfortable and under control in your art space no matter the size of your room. Some of you will be working on a student's desktop, others at your kitchen table. Rest assured that these preparations help to make it comfortable for all. It can be daunting to set up a workspace for creating art, but these lists and tips will make it much easier whether you are working at home or in the classroom. For the little kids, it's most important to find a table and chair that fits their size. Wobbling at a table that is too tall or sitting on their knees makes for a tough beginning. Start with a good fit, relax, and the rest will be easy!

The Master Materials List

A creative place for making art is best fashioned in a comfortable environment—a place free from worry about making a mess. With littler children, the mess concern escalates, and the worry can outweigh the desire to even start creating! If having a special place to make art is not available, you can collect a box of materials, which includes table and floor coverings, and store it in a bin with other toys to be ready to go. This will help eliminate concern and focus the efforts on creativity.

The following list, from simple furnishings to basic materials, will help you get started building your art space or art box. Collecting these supplies over time is easiest and most cost effective, however, you may be surprised how many of these items you already have. When purchasing materials, select student or primary grade. Keep supplies in labeled boxes on shelves for easy storage. Have small containers handy to dispense smaller portions of materials for little hands. Too many choices or too much stuff in the work area can confuse and frustrate smaller children. Most importantly, remember that you don't need all, or even most, of these items to get started! The items are listed loosely by priority.

1. Natural light and/or good overhead lighting—task lighting is appropriate in smaller group situations, such as a clip-on lamp attached to a desk or table for one child.

2. A sturdy table with chairs at the appropriate height for the student—the table should come to about the student's waist when standing, and their feet should be on the floor when seated. If the child is seated on a taller chair at a taller table, provide a sturdy footrest. Many people (of all ages) prefer to stand to make art, just make sure the table is at waist level when standing.

3. A plastic cover is a great way to protect the surface of a multi-use table. Secure the plastic with strong tape if it slips around. Also use a plastic cloth under the table to guard the floor against spills.

4. A water source should be nearby. A sink in the room is best, or provide buckets of water with some empty buckets for dumping the dirty water. A plastic tarp or tablecloth under the buckets helps protect the floor. Collect small and large plastic containers for holding water; round and rectangular are both very useful. Make sure the containers are short walled as little hands have a hard time reaching into tall jars.

5. Remember, washable paint and markers are not completely washable. Wearing a smock or apron is always a good idea with the younger child (and messy adults like me!). Tying back long hair is also a good idea.

6. Newspapers are good for just about everything in the mess control business.

7. Boxes, totes, or shelves to store supplies—label everything to make finding items easier.

8. Plexiglass or Perspex sheets cut to about 8" × 10" (20.5 × 25.5 cm). Provide one sheet for each student to use for printmaking and as a palette for painting. Plexiglass and Perspex sheets last forever and are easy to clean. Plastic egg cartons or small recycled containers are a good for holding paint too.

9. Wax paper and aluminum foil

10. Fiberboard, Masonite, or Plexiglass sheet to support the paper when drawing or painting

11. Rolls of clear tape, masking tape, colored tape, and duct tape

12. Paper of all sorts: 24 lb. (90 gsm) copy paper, 80 lb. (130 gsm) sketching paper, 90 or 140 lb. (190 or 300 gsm) watercolor paper, heavy cardstock, and a collection of fancy colored and printed papers

13. Markers of all colors and thicknesses. Additionally provide black permanent markers, crayons, oil pastels, soft pastels, pencils in a variety of hardness, vine charcoal, colored pencils, kneaded erasers, white plastic erasers, and pencil sharpeners. Large sized crayons and oil pastels are available and recommended.

14. Watercolor pan paints, acrylic paint (both liquid and thick bodied), tempera paint, gouache, and India ink

15. Water-based printmaking ink in black and colors

16. Brayers for rolling the ink when printmaking and doing mixed-media work

17. Brushes in a variety of sizes and shapes: soft haired brushes for watercolor and ink, nylon or bristle brushes for acrylic paint

18. Recycled items, including magazines, greeting cards, candy wrappers, old letters, graph paper, colored wrapping paper, maps, old photographs, discarded artwork, discarded books, stickers, stamp pads, craft sticks, plastic and paper egg cartons, balls of string and yarn, embroidery floss, embroidery hoops, small fabric scraps, cotton swabs, cotton balls, buttons, feathers, textile trims, carded wool, old mats and frames, and polyfoam filling

19. Found objects for printing or texturing paper when drawing. Look for corks, wooden blocks, small sponges, metal washers, lids to spray bottles or cans, corrugated cardboard, lace, craft sticks, pencils with erasers, cookie cutters, straws, plastic toys, tiny cars, cardboard tubes, assorted hardware items, Styrofoam, buttons, and any other items with interesting shapes and textures. Plastic texture plates are available from art suppliers both online and in stores.

20. Adhesives, such as white glue, clear glue, tacky glue, glue sticks for paper, E-6000 extra-strong glue, wood glue, and a hot glue gun with glue sticks. Only the first four listed should be put in the hands of a small child.

21. Canvas boards, canvas paper, stretched canvas, canvas, found wood, smooth birch plywood, mat board, illustration board, cardboard, and fiberboard or Masonite. The wood materials can often be found in scrap piles at lumberyards and frame shops; just ask! All of these should be primed with an acrylic gesso for painting. If the boards are oversized, prime both sides to eliminate any warping.

22. Kitchen supplies helpful in the art process: liquid soap, plastic bowls, wooden spoons, sponges, scrub brushes, drinking straws, old cookie sheets, paper towels, rags, clean recycled foam trays from the grocery store, roll of butcher paper, and plastic cutlery

23. Office supplies including rulers, stapler, paper clips, bull clips, push-pins, rubber stamps, and rubber bands

24. Hardware supplies: hammer, screwdriver, paint-can openers, tape measure, nails, screws, metal washers, sandpaper of varying grit, and foam brushes

25. Store artwork in a cardboard portfolio, old magazine rack, deep drawer, or on a shelf.

26. Provide a display area for finished work, such as a corkboard, string with clips, or wall space!

Basic Methods for Handling Materials in the Studio

Setting Up a Drawing Area

For most drawing lessons, there is little to set up, clean up, and little to spill—with the exception of India ink. Keep India ink in small refillable bottles or shallow containers and always work on newspaper to protect surfaces from the ink.

Keep materials in small containers near the child to keep them engaged. Use muffin tins, recycled containers, or small bowls for drawing supplies.

When using soft pastels or charcoal, have a damp paper towel nearby to keep your fingers clean.

If you are working without a table or outdoors, drawing boards can be made from pieces of Masonite, Plexiglass, or thick foamcore. Use masking tape or bull clips to secure the paper to the surface.

Spray fixatives for charcoal and soft pastels should be used only by an adult and only applied outside. Use a sweeping motion with the can about an arm's length from the paper to keep from spattering.

Setting Up an Area for Painting

Make it a ritual to prepare your workspace in a certain manner so creating is much easier. You can focus on painting when everything is in order, and hopefully you will avoid most accidents.

Protect the table with butcher paper, a plastic tablecloth, or newspaper. Cover the floor with a reusable tarp or plastic tablecloth.

Place a folded sheet of newspaper to the right of your paper if you are right-handed and on the left if you are left-handed—place your water container, brushes, and egg carton paint holder on the newspaper. An extra piece of newspaper folded in half again is good for wiping off water or excess paint. If you set up this way, you will avoid most accidents.

With acrylic paints, dispense coin-size amounts in an egg carton to contain the paint. Keep some of the egg carton sections open for mixing colors. Encourage using a craft stick to mix colors, and supply a different brush for each color. This keeps brush washing to a minimum, water out of the paints, and the paint out of the wash water!

Setting Up an Area for Printmaking

Start your printmaking experience by grabbing a stack of newspaper. Open up five sheets to cover your work area—repeat until you have about ten layers so you can pull away the inky ones and always have a fresh layer underneath as you print. Have a shallow rectangular container of water handy to wash off the brayers when changing colors during the process. Also provide a damp paper towel near the water container to wipe off your fingers if they get too inky.

A Plexiglas palette or foam tray will become your ink station, and a second piece may be used for monotypes. Place your clean printing paper in a stack nearby, but not on your work surface.

Use the brayer to prepare the ink—slowly roll out the ink away from you, in a line the width of your brayer and the length (or less) of your Plexiglass or foam tray. Then pull the brayer back toward you and continue until the ink is smooth. Now you are ready to print!

Use found objects to print with, including corks, wooden blocks, small sponges, metal washers, corrugated cardboard, lace, craft sticks, pencils with erasers, cookie cutters, straws, plastic toys, tiny cars, cardboard tubes, assorted hardware items, Styrofoam, shells, seed pods, old toothbrushes, buttons, or anything else with an interesting shape. Remember—very small children put things in their mouths—make sure that tiny items are well supervised or not used at all.

Tip: Cutting Potatoes for Printing

Use a very sharp knife and cut straight across the potato; blot the potatoes on paper towels to absorb excess juice. Stick a fork into the uncut portion of the potato as a handle, which is good for little hands or slippery produce. Potato stamps can be reused; wash them off, wrap, and store in the refrigerator for up to one week.

Paper & Mixed Media

Collect paper from many sources—from junk mail to beautiful handmade papers. Consider old letters, stamps, wrappers, greeting cards, ticket stubs, old books, dictionaries, wallpaper sample books, graph paper, ledger paper, gift wrap, and cardboard from cereal boxes. Keep your collection in a box and use a small envelope for tiny pieces that are too beautiful to throw away.

Gluing, Tearing & Cutting Paper

To keep your artwork safe and not sticky, use a separate sheet of scrap paper when applying the glue to the paper before sticking it on your artwork.

Tearing and cutting paper produces two different edges. A torn edge is soft and organic; cut paper has a sharp, hard edge.

You can tear your papers in a few different ways. Printed or color paper has special properties—pulling the paper apart from top to bottom with your right hand leading will give the left-hand side a white border. Sometimes a white edge or border is perfect for a special outlined look. Keep your fingers pinched close together for the most controlled tearing.

To tear a straight soft edge, fold the paper where you want to tear it and then fold it back and forth a few more times to break the grain. Press along the fold with a finger and tear the paper along the fold line.

To tear thick handmade paper, first use a wet brush to draw a line where you want to tear and then pull the paper apart.

Cutting paper always gives a crisp edge. If your paper is large you might, want to trim it to a more manageable size before making your actual cuts. Trying to cut a small piece from the middle of the paper is easier if you cut into the spot and then remove the excess around it.

Texture Plates

Texture plates are plastic-patterned plates that can be purchased from most art suppliers. They sometimes lurk in the preschool or clay sections of the store catalog. I have had the same six plates for the past twenty years and use them almost weekly for one thing or another. They can be replaced or used with found objects, such as sneaker or flip-flop soles, coins, combs, leaves, ferns, lace, corrugated cardboard, or anything you can place under a piece of paper and rub over the top with a crayon or oil pastel.

Textiles

Young children love the feel of different fabrics and trims. Keep boxes filled with lace, yarn, material, and buttons. Precut some of the scrap material, yarn, and lace into small shapes because small hands and safety scissors cannot cut these easily. Thread and yarn are easier to handle when they are wound around spools or into small balls. Remember how little their hands are and keep the materials small to fit them!

Clay

Using low fire clay (cone 06-04) is always recommended when working with young children. You can use nontoxic underglazes for color and avoid any of the dangers of higher-fire glazes. Refer to your manual for firing sequences that match the cone rating of your clay. Find a local pottery studio, recreation program, or college to fire the projects if you don't have a kiln.

It is important to keep dust to a minimum—**do not** brush or sweep dried clay. Work on a board or piece of canvas to keep the clay in one place and use a wet sponge to wipe off the surface to keep it clean. Any extra clay should be put back into the original bag. Wash hands with soap and water at the end of a session and *no dry sweeping!*

New clay cut from the bag is fine to use without wedging. Clay that has been used before should be wedged to get rid of any air bubbles before working with it again. To wedge the clay, push the pieces together on a board, and work it similar to kneading bread. Keep pushing the clay and forming a rounded shape, but don't fold it over—you want to get rid of air bubbles, not create more (fig. 1). Air in soda = fizzy fun. Air in clay = broken artwork.

When joining two pieces of clay together, both surfaces must be scored. My friend Megan Bogonovich, a ceramic artist, made these ingenious scoring tools from paint stirrers, epoxy, and sewing pins (fig. 2). They ROCK! They are easy to make and work really well. In the meantime, use any tool, such as a pin tool, to roughen the clay. Scoring tools are sharp—use with care and supervision. Show children the proper way to use the tools and they will respect them. After scoring, add a tiny bit of water on the lines to make a slurry of the clay, push the pieces together, and smooth out the seams.

Fig. 1: *Wedge the clay.*

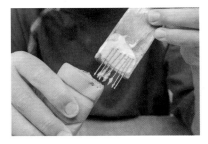

Fig. 2: *A scoring tool roughens the surface.*

Fig. 3: *Paint glaze on the bisqueware.*

When the object is bone dry (not cool to the touch) it is called greenware and can be glazed with velvet underglazes. Greenware is very fragile and must be handled very carefully. I have good luck with small children when glazing greenware by having them only touch the object with their brush, and turn the object by turning the newspaper it is sitting on. The glazes can also be used on bisqueware. Bisqueware is clay after one firing in the kiln, causing the silica to melt and become hard. Use soft brushes to reach all the nooks and crannies when glazing your bisqueware (fig. 3).

Paper Mâché

Using paper mâché is easy. Newspaper and paper towels are the papers of choice for our projects. To make your own paper mâché "goo," start with a cup of flour, and mix in enough water with a fork until it is like thick cream (fig 4). If the project is too wet, simply add dry paper. If it is too dry, add more goo.

Fig. 4: *Paper mâché "goo."*

Drawing

DRAWING IS A NATURAL ACTIVITY for young children to engage in spontaneously. If you have an area set up as an art corner, it is wonderful to have paper and drawing materials readily available for children to use. Store pencils, crayons, oil pastels, and china markers at kid-height so they can help themselves when the mood strikes!

Taking a walk outdoors, exploring a garden or farm, or visiting a city park will open up a treasure box of new ideas for drawing. Even for the busiest child, sitting quietly to notice what's crawling in the grass or what the tree bark of a tree feels like can be a memorable experience. Even on the gloomiest of days, an adventure can be found around your home—in an attic, a toolbox, or when peeling an orange. Helping children to look more closely at the world can be an adventure, a fun way to slow down and, for a moment, step away from our busy lives.

Buttermilk Chalk

- assorted colored chalk
- small container of buttermilk
- 80 lb (216 gsm) white cardstock paper

Tip

For smaller children, fill a plastic egg carton or small recycled cups with a tablespoon or two of buttermilk, and leave a colored piece of chalk in each section to be ready to go.

Go Further

Try making a card for someone special with this method. The buttermilk keeps the chalk vibrant and not too messy.

Think First: Chalk is usually smudgy and dusty. With the addition of buttermilk, chalk turns into a creamy paint-like substance that makes beautiful drawings. Think about shapes you might like to try drawing: Maybe a sunset in the mountains or a design using all the colors you have!

Let's Go!

Fig. 1: *Dip the chalk.*

Fig. 2: *Begin the drawing.*

Fig. 3: *Fill in the drawing.*

1. Begin by dipping the colored chalk into the buttermilk and drawing on your paper (fig. 1).
2. Keep dipping your chalk as you draw to keep the lines creamy and smooth (fig. 2).
3. Continue drawing and dipping the chalk into the buttermilk (fig. 3).
4. For a different option, try white chalk on colored construction paper or cardstock.

Meet the Artist: Albina McPhail

"Painting, to me, is a journey. It is a multi-layered experience of trying to reconcile opposing forces of chance and choice. My work is informed by stepping away from the familiar and desiring to find it again, in however unlikely a form or abstraction. Intent is placed on color, movement, and texture. Relationships between drawing and painting are explored in a search for balance between the controlled and the unpredictable. I find inspiration everywhere, but nature has remained a constant cause of awe and delight."

Grey Matter by Albina McPhail

Crayon Fun

- assorted crayons
- sandpaper, medium grit, cut to desired size
- scissors

optional:

- white cotton fabric or T-shirt
- iron (to be used by an adult)
- white paper
- newsprint paper

Think First: This Lab allows the lighter colors in the crayon box to be the shining stars in the drawing! First choose an idea for the subject matter—most anything works well. A scribble, shapes, flowers, still life, animals—the sky's the limit. Just have your idea ready before you start!

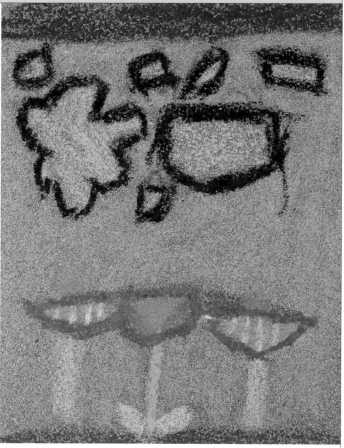

Tip

Younger children can scribble to their hearts content with this lesson. The scribble can be cut into a shape and pressed with an iron onto a white T-shirt to wear with pride!

Go Further

Try a whole series of drawings on sandpaper and then transfer them all to a large piece of white cotton fabric for a wall hanging.

Let's Go!

Fig. 1: Begin the drawing.

3. Continue until the entire piece of sandpaper is covered with your drawing, background included (fig. 3)!

4. Option: You can transfer this drawing onto cotton fabric or T-shirt. Have an adult heat an iron to the highest setting. Lay a sheet of newsprint on the work surface to protect it from any melt through. For a T-shirt, slip the newsprint between the front and back layers. Smooth the fabric on the newsprint, and then place the sandpaper on the fabric with the crayon side facing down. Cover the sandpaper with the white paper, press the hot iron on top, and move slowly all around the white paper. Remove the paper and sandpaper and let cool.

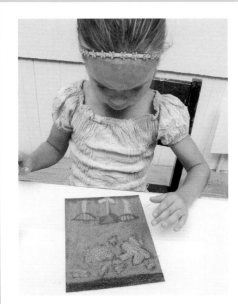

Fig. 3: Fill in the background.

Fig. 2: Press hard enough.

1. Begin your drawing on the rough side of the sandpaper using all the colors you want (fig. 1). Notice how brilliant the colors are!

2. Press hard enough to get the color intensity you want (fig. 2).

Meet the Artist: Jessica Greene

"Constructing a home can be a physical endeavor with nails and wood but it can also be an emotional endeavor using memory and experience to construct a place to rest one's soul. My work is centered around images of both, attempting to find a place in this world to call home, learning to be satisfied with who I am, and build a home inside myself. My use of mixed-media encaustic is a process of layering and constructing in a way that builds the physical pieces along with the imagery."

Insecurity by Jessica Greene

Materials

Think First: This is a fun way to jump-start your imagination and find surprises in your art! There is a lot of fun being free to make marks (or dots) anywhere on your paper. So throw away your concerns about being perfect, and start making dots!

Tip: Younger children may be happiest by simply continuing in black and white. Allow this portion of the lesson to be enough.

- cover stock or other heavy paper
- black permanent marker
- oil pastels or crayons
- watercolor paint
- watercolor brush
- newspaper
- wash water

Go Further

- Try using a different colored permanent marker as artist Ashley Goldberg did in her picture.
- Make the dots with a friend on one piece of paper, and then complete the drawing together—collaborative art is fun!

Let's Go!

Fig. 1: *Make lots of dots.*

Fig. 3: *Each artist's work is different!*

Fig. 4: *Begin to add color.*

Fig. 2: *Connect the dots.*

4. Notice that your drawing and your friend's drawings are different (fig. 3).

5. Begin adding color to your drawing with oil pastels or watercolors (fig. 4).

6. Finish adding color as you like (fig. 5) and try this Lab again!

Fig. 5: *Finish the color.*

1. Using the permanent marker, make small dots all over your paper in any fashion you choose (fig. 1). Remember—there is no wrong way!

2. When you have plenty of dots on your paper, stop! Take a look at what you have done.

3. Find something inside your dots—what if they were connected one way or another? Begin to connect them to create your new found image (fig. 2).

Meet the Artist: Ashley Goldberg

Ashley Goldberg is an artist living in Portland, Oregon. She has loved arts, crafts, creatures, and nature her entire life. Her artwork is simple, but with a sophisticated color palette. Ashley believes great emotion can be conveyed in a simple gesture or look. The characters she creates, often monsters or little girls, are simple, humorous, empathetic, and a little bit pathetic. Learn more about Ashley's work at www.etsy.com/people/ashleyg.

Progress by Ashley Goldberg

Oil Pastels

- oil pastels
- white drawing paper

Go Further

Add watercolor to your oil pastel drawing if you would like to try that.

Think First: Choose objects for a still life that are interesting to you and that you are familiar with. Feel the items and examine them up close. Arrange everything in front of you the way you would like to draw them. Oil pastels are fun to draw with because you can blend the colors as you would with paint!

Tip: For younger children, encourage smudging some of the primary colors (red, yellow, and blue) together with their finger for some color mixing fun.

Let's Go!

Fig. 1: *Begin the drawing.*

Fig. 2: *Look carefully.*

Fig. 3: *Add the colors.*

1. Using the oil pastels, begin drawing any of the objects in front of you (fig. 1).
2. Keep your eyes on the shapes of your objects as you draw (fig. 2).
3. Use all the colors you see in the objects for your drawing (fig. 3). You are the artist, so you choose the colors!
4. Continue your drawing using all the colors you see.
5. Add a background if you want—draw what you see or use your imagination.
6. When you are finished, step back from your drawing and admire it!

Meet the Artist: Judith Andrews

Judith Andrews is a painter from Eliot, Maine. "Cultivated by a lifetime of immersion in the natural world, I make use of images and icons, along with my own intrinsic sense of shape, color, and texture to support imaginary landscape and still life work." Learn more about Judith Andrews at www.judithandrews. squarespace.com.

Overboard by Judith Andrews

Ice Drawings

Think First: Begin by filling an ice cube tray with water. Select the food coloring that you would like to use, and drop four to six drops into each section. Once the tray is filled, put it into the freezer. When the water is half frozen, place a craft stick into each section to serve as handles for the "color cubes." Leave some cubes without sticks to use directly with your hands.

- white cover stock
- food coloring
- craft sticks
- prepared ice cubes
  (see "Think First")
- egg carton

Tip

Younger children may prefer to use cubes without sticks. Encourage them to make broad motions with their arm for wide strokes.

Go Further

Try drawing with your color cubes over a crayon or oil-pastel drawing to see what happens!

Let's Go!

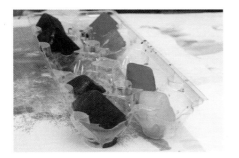

Fig. 1: Use an egg carton to hold cubes.

1. Release the color cubes from the tray and put them into egg carton sections as a holder (fig. 1).

2. Choose a subject to draw, such as an abstract, portrait, still life, or landscape, and start drawing (fig. 2).

3. Try making new colors by layering one color over the other (fig. 3).

4. Use as many colors as you like, overlapping them and making new colors as you go.

Fig. 2: Begin the drawing.

Meet the Author: Susan Schwake

"This watercolor illustration was inspired by my fondness for hedgehogs. It would be sad to see them out in the snow because there would be nothing to eat! I just thought they would look great making little footprints and foraging in the woods in December." Learn more about Susan's work at www.susanschwake.com.

December by Susan Schwake

Fig. 3: Layer to make new colors.

Ink Spots

Think First: Ink is by nature a messy material if spilled. Protect your work surface with paper or a covering that you can easily wipe up—just in case! For the very youngest child, an adult can fill the dropper, and then the child can make the spots. Learning to fill a dropper can be endless fun!

Tip: The younger child may not be able to blow though a straw with a lot of success. I suggest they pick up the paper and tip it from side to side to make the ink run.

- ink with dropper (black or colored ink)
- cover stock
- oil pastels
- drinking straw

Go Further

- If you like watercolor painting, you can use paint instead of oil pastels to finish your drawing.
- Try an old-fashioned quill pen—they are exciting to use! Dip into colored ink, and then follow the edges and fill in the spaces.

Let's Go!

Fig. 1: Drop the ink spots.

Fig. 2: Blow the ink with a straw.

1. Fill your ink dropper by squeezing the rubber, inserting the tube into the ink, and then letting go to fill.
2. Gently drop ink spots one at a time onto your paper wherever you would like them to be (fig. 1).
3. Take a straw and blow through it to push the ink around (fig. 2). A short blast of air with the end of the straw close to the paper works best.
4. Let the spots dry.
5. Using the oil pastels, connect your spots by either filling in the white space between them or drawing around the spots by following their shapes (fig. 3).

Fig. 3: Draw with oil pastels.

Meet the Artist: Tim Wirth

Tim Wirth builds square paintings that explore color, shape, and imagery in deceptively simple ways. His distinctive craftsmanship and the combinations of tension, intrigue, and humor in his work have captured the interest of various collectors and critics, including the Brooklyn Rail founder and publisher Phong Bui, renowned art scholar and historian Karen Wilkin, and the legendary singer/songwriter John Mellencamp. His work is in public and private collections across the country and has been exhibited internationally. Learn more about his artwork at www.TimWirth.com.

Untitled (You Can Go Your Own Way Now) by Tim Wirth

Ink & Cotton Swabs

- drawing paper
- India ink in small nonspill bottle
- cotton swabs

Think First: Play around and try making many different marks with the cotton swab. Don't overload your swab with ink. Move your arm around freely to make broad strokes.

Tip: Make sure that younger children wear smocks that don't drag into their artwork. Smooth fitting long sleeves go a long way in this project!

Go Further

Try drawing on a page from a discarded book as our artist Darryl Joel Berger did. He used an old math textbook page.

Let's Go!

Fig. 1: *Dip the swab in ink.*

Fig. 3: *Make some lines.*

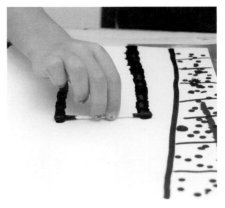

Fig. 4: *Try rolling the swab.*

Fig. 2: *Make dots.*

1. Begin by loading your swab with ink (fig. 1).
2. Try making dots first (fig. 2).
3. Try making lines (fig. 3).
4. Try rolling the swab with both ends full of ink (fig. 4).
5. Use these methods and create a drawing of your choice.

Meet the Artist: Darryl Joel Berger

I asked Darryl to tell us how he draws with ink. "I don't make any preparatory marks with pencil—I just dip my Chinese brush into a small well of ink and start drawing directly onto the paper. This is the beauty of the drawing in ink: direct and fluid, with no scratching around beforehand. You should not be mimicking holding a pencil or pen, but it's not exactly like holding a regular painting brush either—it's somewhere in between. When I draw in ink I like to start very wet, at the picture's darkest spots, and keep going until the brush dries a bit, and then the looser brush hairs will give you some wonderful effects. The best ink drawings are gestural and graphic all at once (just like Chinese characters)." More information about Darryl can be found at www.darryljoelberger.tumblr.com.

Choisie by Darryl Joel Berger

Materials

- canvas or other heavyweight fabric
- pencil and drawing paper
- assortment of oil pastels
- masking tape
- still life objects for reference if desired

Tip

Younger children should be encouraged to skip the paper–sketch step and draw their ideas directly on the fabric.

Go Further

- It would be fun and challenging to make a wall hanging with portraits of your family. Each square could be one portrait. An adult could help sew them together into a wall hanging.

- Try an abstract doodle design starting with black and then fill in the spaces with bright colors!

Think First: Decide what you would like to draw. For this Lab, the artist chose a bird as the subject matter. Sketch out a few ideas on paper to get your ideas flowing if you like. Cut the sketch paper the same size as your fabric so you know how big the drawing will actually be. If you don't have an idea, try choosing a few items around the room that look interesting to you, and arrange them into a still life.

Let's Go!

Fig. 1: Begin with oil pastels.

1. Sketch your ideas on paper with pencil if desired. Tape down the fabric edges so it doesn't move around while you draw.
2. Begin drawing your subject matter with the oil pastels (fig. 1).
3. Continue drawing to create your image (fig. 2).
4. Don't forget to add a background; it gives your subject matter a place to live (fig. 3).

Fig. 2: Continue the drawing.

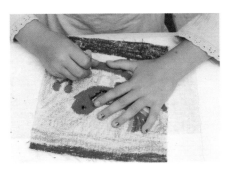

Fig. 3: Fill in the background.

Meet the Artist: Matt Wyatt

Matt Wyatt is an abstract expressionist and photographer. His work has been exhibited in a variety of venues and has received regional and national attention. He resides in New Hampshire and serves as the president of the Rochester Museum of Fine Arts. More about Matt can be found at www.rochestermfa.org.

Home on the Range by Matt Wyatt

LAB 9 Marble Drawing

Materials

- cardstock
- three colors of acrylic or tempera paint
- small containers for paint
- three marbles
- box with low sides

Think First: Choose three colors of paint that you like. Think about trying this lesson a few times with different color combinations. You can use three colors, let them dry, and then add three additional colors. Marble drawing is fun for people of all ages!

Go Further

In good weather, you can do this project outdoors with a really large piece of paper (perhaps from a roll of paper) and tennis balls. Dip the balls into the paint, and then bounce or roll them along the paper to draw your colorful lines.

Tip

This lesson can be a collaboration between a very young child and an adult, or between two young children. Use a larger box with short sides and let each artist take a side. Rolling the marbles around together is a lot of fun. Make sure that they make two of each drawing—one for each artist!

Let's Go!

Fig. 1: *Cut paper to fit.*

Fig. 2: *Put marbles in the paint.*

1. Add some paint to each small container. Cut the cardstock to fit inside the box (fig. 1).

2. Drop a marble into each container of paint (fig. 2).

3. Remove the marbles from the paint and drop them into the box. Tip the box back and forth to make the marbles roll around the paper (fig. 3).

4. Continue tipping the box to make new lines over the first lines and create new colors (fig. 4)!

5. Let the marbles roll around the box, mixing the paint as they go. You can dip them into the paint again as they run out of color.

Fig. 3: *Tip the box.*

Fig. 4: *Continue the drawing.*

Meet the Author: Susan Schwake

"Many times my painting process starts with drawing and texturing lines in the background or bottom layers. These layers peek through in the end and the effect is exactly what I am looking for—texture, spontaneous line, and color."

Fence Hopping by Susan Schwake

Tape Flags

- assorted colored paper-tape rolls
- scissors
- cardboard tube to hold tapes
- white cover stock

optional:

- watercolors
- brushes
- wash water

Think First: This Lab allows the tape to make the lines instead of drawing them. Search online or at your local library to see different flags of the world. Decide what colors to use and get ideas for your design. Sketch your flag out ahead if desired, or simply begin!

Tip

Younger children will be frustrated by trying to cut tape from a roll. Help them along by tearing or cutting multiple strips and lightly attaching them to the table's edge. This way they can grab what they need. Do let them try tearing the tapes when they are ready though.

Go Further

- You can make different shaped flags by first cutting your paper to the desired form.
- A number of flags could be attached to a string and hung across a doorway or wall.

Let's Go!

Fig. 1: *Pull off a piece of tape.*

Fig. 2: *Cut from the paper tube.*

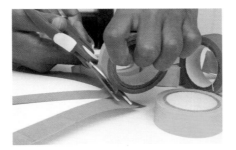

Fig. 3: *Cut from the tape roll.*

Fig. 4: *Smooth the tape.*

Fig. 5: *Add small pieces of tape.*

1. Start by pulling off your first section of colored tape (fig. 1).

2. Find what is easier for you: pulling the tape from the cardboard tube and cutting (fig. 2), or pulling it from a single roll (fig. 3). Some children will need help cutting the tape. You could also hold the tape and let them try cutting.

3. Use your fingers to smooth the tape down on the paper as you go (fig. 4).

4. Tear small pieces of tape and press them onto the flag for additional decorations (fig. 5).

5. Just use tape, or finish your flag with watercolors if you desire.

Meet the Artist: Jasper Johns

Jasper Johns is a well-known American artist who may be best known for his paintings of flags. This particular painting is done in encaustic (wax) and depicts the American flag. More information on Jasper Johns is available at www.jasperjohns.com.

Flag, 1954, by Jasper Johns

Painting

I BELIEVE THAT PAINTING is something all children love to do. Some love it more than others, but I have never had a child refuse to paint when offered the chance. These lessons run the gamut from experimental to a more controlled outcome—all with endless possibilities. I chose lessons I have found over the past twenty years to be most valuable for many different ages. So these are lessons to grow with, to repeat, and to see what wonderful new ideas can emerge. I am a great lover of good materials, so even though your littles are young, break out the best paints you can for these lessons. You never know what will happen!

UNIT 3

Spray-Bottle Paintings

Think First: When using extra water in a painting project you want to start with enough paint on your brush—be mindful of this as you go along. Reload your brush with color and don't be afraid to splash it around your painting a bit! This is a spontaneous painting lesson with different results every time.

Tip: This lesson is perfect for younger children. Just be sure that the spray bottle is one they can operate easily.

- watercolors
- heavyweight watercolor paper
- small spray bottle filled with water
- wash water
- newspaper

Go Further

Try using only primary colors so they mix into secondary colors as you spray.

Let's Go!

Fig. 1: *Begin with the first color.*

Fig. 3: *Tip the paper.*

Fig. 2: *Spray the painting with water.*

Fig. 4: *Blot extra water.*

1. Wet your brush and choose a color to begin. Load the brush with a lot of color (fig. 1).
2. Continue with lots of colors and free painting on your paper. Don't try to make a specific subject as the paint will move when you spray it with water.
3. Spray your painting with the spray bottle (fig. 2).

4. Continue to paint or spray as desired. Tip the paper to run the water around the painting (fig. 3).
5. Blot the paper if desired with a paper towel to change the amount of water left to dry (fig. 4); let dry!

Meet the Author: Susan Schwake

This watercolor painting used the wet-on-wet technique for parts of the background. This method is unpredictable and similar to the spray-bottle method. To see more of the author's paintings, visit www.susanschwake.com.

Bird Picnic by Susan Schwake

Pick a Brush

- assorted paintbrushes
- watercolors
- paper
- wash water
- newspaper

Think First: It's good to know what kind of marks your brushes will make, so this Lab helps you explore the wonderful world of your brushes—you are going to be a brush detective! Look through your supplies and pull out all of your brushes. Look at how the hairs are shaped. Try and guess what kind of line each brush will make before you begin.

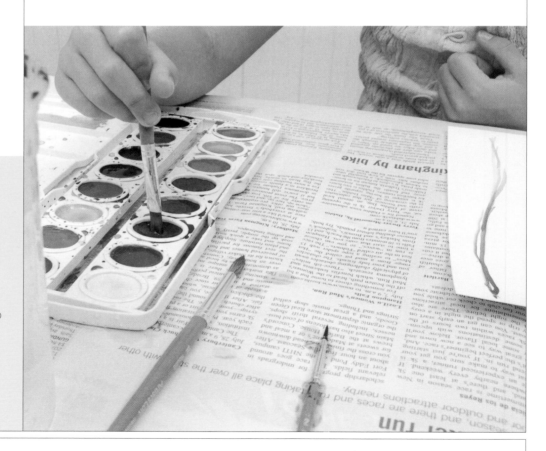

Tip

This Lab works well for the youngest child by using larger brushes. Have them try making the lines on larger paper taped to a wall if possible.

Go Further

You may want to label your paintings to remember which brush made the different lines. Keep the paintings to remind you what each brush can do!

Let's Go!

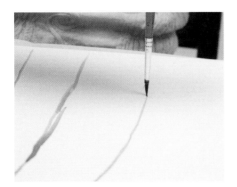

Fig. 1: Start with the first brush.

Fig. 2: Try out all the brushes.

Fig. 3: Observe the shape of the lines .

Fig. 4: Make dots.

1. Choose a brush, wet it, and select a color to begin. Make a series of lines with the brush (fig. 1).
2. Continue the exploration of each brush by making more lines on your paper (fig. 2).
3. As you paint, observe the line each brush makes (fig. 3).

4. Try making dots with the brushes on another piece of paper (fig. 4). Hold the brush close to the bristles to paint, and then try holding the end of the handle. See what happens!
5. Use all of your brushes in this fashion to become more familiar with what your tools will do.

Meet the Artist: Paul Klee

Paul Klee was an artist from Switzerland who was part of a modern movement of artists during World War I. His works are considered childlike and were often created with many media including oils and watercolor. His use of watercolor is delicate and beautiful. Learn more about this artist at en.wikipedia.org/wiki/Paul_Klee.

"Art does not reproduce the visible; rather, it makes visible." —Paul Klee

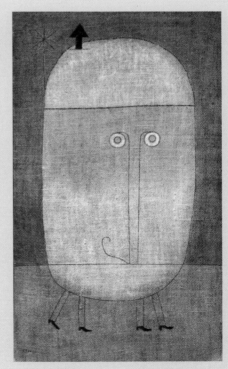

Mask of Fear, (oil on burlap) by Paul Klee

Watercolor Magic

- white oil pastel
- watercolor paper
- small sponge
- watercolors
- water
- wash water
- newspaper
- coarse salt

Think First: Think about a night scene or a snowy landscape that you would like to draw. Will there be stars? Falling snow? What form is the land? Are there mountains or hills? Is it the desert? You choose and think it through before you begin.

Tip: This lesson can be adapted for young children by allowing them to choose their subject matter without prompting, and let them draw freely with white oil pastel. Even a scribble will be magical in the end. Encourage using darker or saturated watercolors for the best effects!

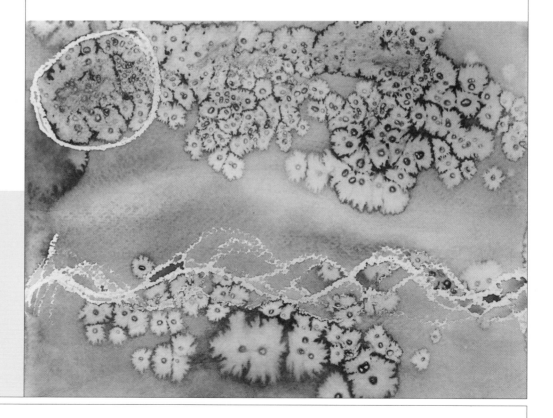

Go Further

Try using all the colors in the oil pastel box and plenty of saturated watercolor to create a painting that has texture where you place the salt. For example, create colorful rocks, underwater coral reefs, or textured fish.

Let's Go!

Fig. 1: Begin with the oil pastel.

Fig. 2: Wet paper with the water.

Fig. 3: Paint with the watercolor.

Fig. 4: Sprinkle the salt.

1. Start with the oil pastel and draw your subject matter (fig. 1).
2. When your drawing is finished, wet the paper with a small sponge (fig. 2).
3. Use plenty of water when painting with watercolor (fig. 3). The paper should be extra wet to accept the salt. Notice how the white oil-pastel lines are not disturbed by the paint!
4. When finished, give the child a dish of salt so they may "pinch" and sprinkle it sparingly on their painting (fig. 4). Use the salt for snowflakes or stars. A little goes a long way!
5. Let the painting dry and brush off the salt. Notice the effects the salt had—magic!

Meet the Artist: August Macke

August Macke was a German artist who created work in oils and watercolors. He was a painter of the Expressionism movement and some of his later work was considered Fauvist. His rich colors and shapes are part of all of his works. For more information on Macke visit www.augustmacke.org.

Kairouan III by August Macke, 1914

Drip, Drop, Splat!

- cover stock or other heavy paper
- watercolor brush
- watercolor paint
- newspaper
- wash water

Think First: Students enjoy this lesson more than any I have ever taught. For this Lab, we will explore the indoor splatter-painting techniques so protect your area with plenty of newspaper. If you are able to work outside, you can use your whole arm to splatter the paint!

Tip: Littles just love splatter. Protect them with smocks and the work area with drop cloths. Let the paint fly! Outdoors is always the best choice for the littlest of splatter artists.

Go Further

- These finished papers can be cut or folded to make beautiful greeting cards or postcards to send to your friends.
- Try using primary colors (red, yellow, and blue) to encourage spontaneous color mixing.

Let's Go!

Fig. 1: *Get paint on the brush.*

Fig. 2: *Tap the brush.*

Fig. 3: *It can get messy!*

Fig. 4: *Add more colors.*

Meet the Artist: Jackson Pollock

Jackson Pollock was a famous American painter known for his action paintings. He was the first painter to abandon brushes and pour, drip, and splatter his paint onto his canvases. His *Lavender Mist* painting was considered one of his most ambitious works. Learn more about Jackson Pollock at www.moma.org.

Number 1, Lavender Mist
by Jackson Pollock

1. Lay down plenty of newspaper in your work area.

2. Dip your brush in the water and keep it very wet. Dip the brush into your first color choice (fig. 1).

3. Hold the brush over your paper and gently tap it with one finger (fig. 2). Keep repeating this step until you want to change colors. Remember to wash your brush between colors.

4. Splatter painting can get messy (fig. 3), but you can wash up at the end.

5. Use as many colors as you like until your paper is covered! Notice how the colors mix on your paper to make new colors (fig. 4).

Mixing It Up

- white cover stock
- watercolor paints in primary colors
- watercolor brushes
- wash water for brushes
- newspaper

Think First: Do you ever wonder where all the colors come from? It's always fun to learn by doing, and when you "do" with paint, it's exciting! This Lab is all about exploring the color wheel by making new colors. If you can get a copy of *Little Blue and Little Yellow* by Leo Lionni, read it to your young artists before beginning the lesson.

Tip: For the littlest paint mixers, try one brush for each color and use a flattened coffee filter or other absorbent paper to paint on instead of card stock or watercolor paper. It keeps things fun, puddles to a minimum, and the colors blend easily.

Go Further

Try mixing your three new colors with one of the original colors you started with. What happens?

Let's Go!

Fig. 1: Paint a puddle.

Fig. 2: Add the yellow puddle.

Fig. 3: Swirl the colors together.

5. Wash your brush again. Try mixing red and yellow to make a new color. Wash your brush and then try red and blue. You will make three new colors from the three you began with (fig. 4).

Fig. 4: Make three new colors!

1. Start with a very wet brush and pick up the color blue.
2. Make a nice puddle of blue paint on your paper (fig. 1).
3. Wash your brush, and then pick up the color yellow. Make a yellow puddle below the blue puddle with a space in between (fig. 2).
4. Pull some of the yellow into the space between the puddles. Then pull in some blue and swirl your brush around (fig. 3).

Meet the Artist: Leo Lionni

Leo Lionni was a celebrated children's author. His books are still among my favorites. His first book was *Little Blue and Little Yellow* which he made up for his children during a long train ride. Our family dearly loves every book he wrote. Explore more of his books at your local library or look online at www.randomhouse.com/kids/lionni.

Little Blue and Little Yellow by Leo Lionni

little blue and little yellow

by Leo Lionni

Cotton Ball Color

- bag of cotton balls
- cotton swabs
- tempera paints
- white cardstock
- foam tray or egg carton for paints

Think First: This Lab explores color instead of shape by mixing colors on the painting and being bold without a brush. Choose your colors before you start—think about what might mix into new colors. Feel free to add white into the mix to make some pastel colors.

Tip: This is a fun lesson for the very young. Taking their cue from you, they can dip and dab just like the big kids. As they add more colors to their page, have them stop occasionally and look at what has happened so far.

Go Further

- Try painting on a colored sheet of paper.
- Use white or clear glue and add the colorful cotton balls to the painting when they are dry.

Let's Go!

Fig. 1: Dip into the paint.

Fig. 2: Dab on the color.

Fig. 3: Add more color.

Fig. 4: Add small dots of color.

Meet the Artist: Ashley Goldberg

Oregon artist Ashley Goldberg has loved arts, crafts, creatures, and nature all her life. Focusing on portraiture and capturing a brief moment in time, her artwork is simple, but with a sophisticated color palette. Ashley believes great emotion can be conveyed with a simple gesture or look. The characters she creates are simple, humorous, empathetic, and a little bit pathetic. Learn more about Ashley's work at www.etsy.com/people/ashleyg.

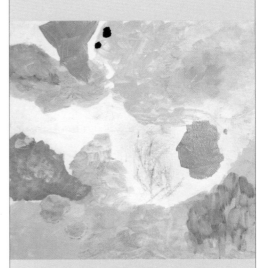

Untitled by Ashley Goldberg

1. Dispense the paints into an egg carton.
2. Dip a cotton ball into the paint (fig. 1).
3. Begin dabbing or dragging the cotton ball on your paper (fig. 2).
4. Use the other colors and keep dabbing and mixing colors as you go (fig. 3).
5. Add smaller dots with cotton swabs if you desire (fig. 4).
6. Let the paint dry and try another color or call it finished!

That's Not a Brush!

Materials

Materials

- sponge bottle washer
- tempera paints
- white cardstock
- foam tray
- sink or bucket to wash the bottle washer

Go Further

- Try bouncing the brush on a black or colored sheet of paper. We used black paper for contrast.

- These paintings are beautiful as they are, or they can be cut up and used in the mixed-media Labs in this book.

Painting on black paper

Think First: This Lab will hopefully start you on an adventure of exploring non-artist materials. I have found that some common household items make interesting paintbrush substitutes. This Lab uses my favorite—the foam bottle washer! Choose your paints and painting tool—use what you have on hand and what you learned about color mixing in "Lab 15."

Tip: All small children love to paint with sponges, so let the very youngest try this lesson. Help them dip the sponge into the paint until they get the hang of it.

Let's Go!

Fig. 1: *Dip into the paint.*

1. Dispense your paints onto a foam tray.
2. Dip one side of your tool into one color and the other side into another color (fig. 1).
3. Begin bouncing the paint-filled tool onto your paper (fig. 2). Have fun—it's bouncy!

Fig. 2: *Bounce on the color.*

4. Continue with more paint and more bouncing (fig. 3).
5. Let dry and admire your work, or cut it up to make a collage as shown.

Fig. 3: *Add more color.*

Meet the Artist: Mati Rose McDonough

Mati Rose McDonough is an adult who paints like a child. It has taken her thirty-two years, two schools, and approximately 486 paintings to get to this point. Mati is inspired by beauty, truth, lies, urban animals perched in trees, bits of eavesdropped conversation, young imaginations, faded signs, the ocean, patchwork quilts, ornate ironwork, ice-cream carts, and stories of longing. Learn more about Mati Rose at www.matirose.com.

Little Seal by Mati Rose McDonough

Materials

- oil pastels
- watercolor
- brushes
- small wooden board (primed) or small canvas board
- black permanent marker

Think First: Look at your house and sketch out a drawing, or snap a photo to work from. Working from memory is fine too! Think about how many windows and doors your house has. What does the yard look like? Ask yourself these questions.

Tip

Give the youngest child a pencil to use on the board and then the oil pastels. At the end, they can use a black oil pastel to trace shapes if they desire. Show them how to smudge with their fingers to blend the colors.

Go Further

- Try painting your favorite friend's house or maybe your relative's house. These make great gifts!
- Maybe you are more interested in your backyard. Try painting that without your house!

Let's Go!

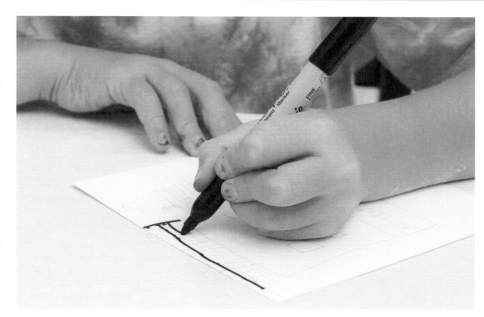

Fig. 1: Draw the house.

1. Use the black marker to draw your house on the board (fig. 1). You may start with pencil if you wish, and then go over it with the marker.

2. Use oil pastels to add color to the house and yard (fig. 2).

3. Finish the painting with watercolor. The oil pastel will resist the watercolor, and the lines will stay intact.

Fig. 2: Add the color.

Meet the Artist: Lindy Carroll

Lindy Carroll is a painter from Newmarket, New Hampshire. She holds a MFA in painting from the University of New Hampshire. Her paintings are delicate renditions of areas around New England and beyond.

Backyard View by Lindy Carroll

Sweet Paintings

Materials

- small can of sweetened condensed milk
- liquid watercolors, ink, or liquid pigments
- spoon
- cover stock
- brushes

Think First: This Lab allows a young child to work in a thick enamel-like paint without the toxic side effects. The sweetened condensed milk adds a texture and gloss to the paint with a result like no other child-safe paint. It's sticky, gooey, and a whole lot of fun. Let the painting dry completely before moving it.

Tip

Make sure the paint goes on the paper and not in the mouth of the youngest child.

Go Further

Try using this paint on a wooden surface. Use recycled wood or scraps from from a lumberyard or local carpenter.

Let's Go!

Fig. 1: *Mix the paint.*

Fig. 2: *Begin the painting.*

Fig. 3: *Mix new colors on your paper.*

Meet the Artist:
Mitchell Rosenzweig

Mitchell is an artist who splits his time between New Jersey and New Mexico. Mitchell says, "The heavily abstracted landscape imagery has always been the central theme in my paintings; I enjoy the challenge of translating nature into abstraction." The painting *Double Dome* is rendered in enamel and oil paint. Learn more about Mitchell Rosenzweig at www.mitchellrosenzweig.com.

Double Dome by Mitchell Rosenzweig

1. Mix up your paint in small containers; we used a plastic egg carton, but any small recycled dish will work. Pour a small amount of the milk into your container, add a few drops of color, and mix until it is one solid color (fig. 1).

2. Decide your painting's subject matter.

3. Begin painting with your first color (fig. 2).

4. Continue your painting using all the colors you have. Try mixing new colors in a fresh container (fig. 3).

Op Art

Materials

- oil pastels
- white drawing paper
- watercolor paints
- newspaper
- wash water

Think First: Take a peek at a few of the artists from the Op Art movement. Find information about these optical-illusion artists at your local library. In this Lab, we are going to play with the same shapes these artists used: rectangles and circles. Choose the colors of oil pastels to use ahead of time.

Tip: This is a great way to get the very young child interested in shapes. Use objects to trace around that are shaped the same as what you want to draw, such as a small jewelry box for rectangles or a plastic cup for a circle. They can make the additional shapes inside (smaller) and outside (larger).

Go Further

These Op Art paintings could be done on small matt board pieces, and then made into a mobile as described in the "Unit 5" sculpture section.

Let's Go!

Fig. 1: Repeat drawing your shape.

1. Begin drawing either circles or rectangles with the oil pastels. Start either in the middle or around the outside edge of the paper.
2. Continue going around and around your chosen shape (inside if you started on the edge, or outside if you started in the middle) until the drawing is complete (fig. 1).
3. Paint with as many colors as you like to fill in the white spaces left on the painting (fig. 2).
4. Finish your painting, and then try a different shape (fig. 3)!

Fig. 2: Paint over the oil pastel.

Fig. 3: Finish your painting.

Meet the Artist: Victor Vasarely

Victor Vasarely is considered the father of "Op Art." His works are in art museums around the world, and his work in the 1960s and '70s has been credited to have impacted fashion, computer science, and architecture. More information on Victor Vasarely can be found at www.vasarely.com.

Shown at right is an Op Art sculpture by Victor Vasarely in Pécs, Hungary.

LAB 21 Circle Paintings

Materials

- large sheet of colored construction paper
- large, round profile brush
- three colors of acrylic or tempera paint
- white acrylic or tempera paint
- newspaper
- wash water

Meet the Artist: Wassily Kandinsky

Wassily Kandinsky was born in Moscow and lived part of his life in Germany and then France. His work changed greatly during his life, and his work in abstract expressionism is most recognized. He used shapes—such as the circle—to express his inner life as an artist.

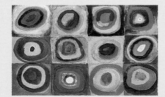

Farbstudie Quadrate
by Wassily Kandinsky

Think First: Circles are a natural, familiar shape for children. They (as well as adults) enjoy making them. Before beginning this lesson, you can ask the child to make circles in the air with one finger, then with their whole arm, and finally to make a circle with their hands stretched out spinning around in a circle. This lesson focuses on composition through art making, by way of the color, value, and subject of the painting being predetermined.

Tip: For the youngest child, make sure they can reach most of the paper from where they are standing. This may mean a smaller piece of paper.

Let's Go!

Fig. 1: Use the first color.

Fig. 2: Add the second color.

Fig. 3: Use the third color.

1. Starting with one of the colors you have chosen, make circles all over your paper. If you wish, you can make some of them dots (filled in circles). Any size is fine (fig. 1).

2. Wash out the brush and dry thoroughly.

3. Choose a second color and start making new circles and dots on your paper. Fill in some of the first circles if you like or outline existing circles (fig. 2).

4. Continue the painting with the third color. Paint in some of the background and outline circles you have already made (fig. 3).

5. Finally, use the white to outline circles, fill in circles, or fill in the background. If you already used white, use one of the remaining colors (fig. 4).

Fig. 4: Fill the background.

Go Further

Try painting other shapes in this fashion.

Printmaking

MAKING MULTIPLE ART IMAGES is an addictive process. Printmaking is instant gratification with the element of chance enhancing the technical process. Very young children love to make hand prints or finger prints—just watch them with pudding on a highchair tray! These Labs will allow further exploration using different papers and a variety of methods to produce endless variations from each Lab.

UNIT 4

Letter Prints

- foam letter stamps
- paint
- foam tray
- cardstock

Think First: These prints use letter shapes to form a picture, such as a landscape with hills, a building, or perhaps a person or animal. Let the child's imagination run wild!

Tip

Printing with alphabet letters can introduce children to their forms and begin letter recognition.

Go Further

Try to fill the whole paper with printed letters and still be able to see your subject matter.

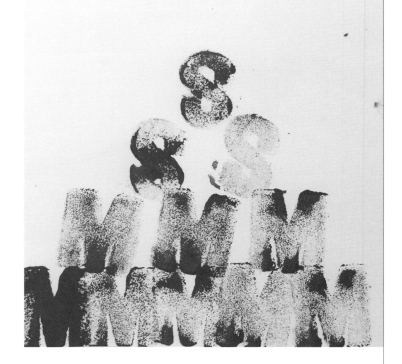

Let's Go!

Fig. 1: Arrange the letters.

Fig. 2: Print with the foam letter.

Fig. 3: Dip and print.

Fig. 4: Complete your shape.

1. Arrange the letters into the shapes you want to create (fig. 1).

2. Dip your letters into the paint and blot some of the excess paint on the side of the tray. Print your first letter (fig. 2).

3. Continue dipping and printing to create a subject or shape with the letters (fig. 3).

4. Complete printing your shape (fig. 4). If desired, fill in the background using only the letters. They can be upside down, sideways, and right side up.

Meet the Artist: Robert Indiana

Robert Indiana is an American artist who often uses words in his paintings. His *Love* painting was used by the United States Post Office in their first in a series of love stamps. Find more on Robert Indiana's work at www.robertindiana.com.

Love Stamp by Robert Indiana

Fold Me a Print

- cover stock
- paintbrush
- acrylic or tempera paint
- newspaper
- Plexiglas for palette
- wash water

Think First: These spontaneous prints are a great way to experience mirror images. It's a playful way to introduce young children to printmaking and will consume more than a few minutes with the process. Have the children choose the colors and help them prefold the paper until they can do it by themselves.

Tip

A very young child might dispense the paint more easily with a small squeeze bottle. Try recycling a small glue bottle and fill it with liquid tempera paint for this process.

Go Further

- Try making a face, rainbow, or butterfly with this method.
- Start with just blobs of paint and see what you find when you open up the paper!

Let's Go!

Fig. 1: Prefold your paper.

Fig. 2: Paint to the left of the fold.

1. Fold the paper in half. Open up the paper and lay it flat (fig. 1).
2. Pick up some paint with the brush and paint on ONE side of the fold (fig. 2).
3. Finish painting and then refold the paper (fig. 3).
4. Press and firmly rub the closed paper (fig. 4).
5. Open and peek inside (fig. 5)!
6. Continue painting, folding, and peeking until you are finished with the print (fig. 6).

Fig. 3: Fold the paper.

Fig. 4: Rub the folded paper.

Fig. 5: Peek inside!

Fig. 6: Continue adding to your print.

Meet the Author:
Susan Schwake

"I am often fascinated by the role chance can play within an artwork. I created this body of work labeled *Untitled* to exhaust that role of chance. The reason for keeping the works numbered and untitled was to keep the viewer interacting with the piece—allowing them to see what they like in the work." Learn more about Susan Schwake at www.susanschwake.com.

Untitled IV by Susan Schwake

Spuds!

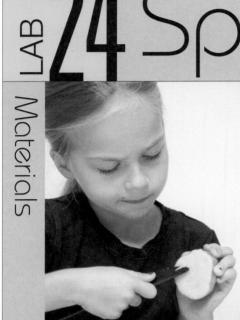

Think First: An adult should cut the potatoes in half with a sharp knife. Make sure to cut straight across to create a flat surface for the best prints.

Tip: Small hands will have better control if you stick a fork in the back of the potato as a handle.

- small round potatoes
- assorted colored ink pads
- cover stock
- colored papers
- absorbent paper towels
- newspapers
- plastic knife
- forks (plastic or metal)

Go Further

You can make greeting cards and wrapping paper with potato prints!

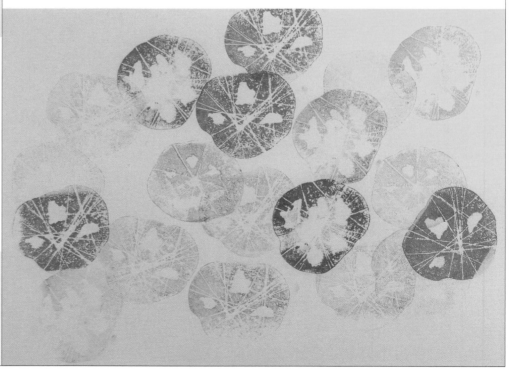

Let's Go!

Fig. 1: *Begin making lines.*

Fig. 2: *Make round divots.*

Fig. 3: *Press the potato in the ink.*

Fig. 4: *Stamp onto the paper.*

Meet the Artist: Friedensreich Hundertwasser

Hundertwasser was a well-known artist born in Austria. His work ranged from architecture to paintings and even stamps as we see here. He never used straight lines, and circles were very important to him. His colorful building in Vienna, Austria, is an amazing display of his unique work. For more information on Hundertwasser visit: www.hundertwasser.at.

UN Stamp by Hundertwasser

1. To make a line across the potato, saw back and forth on the cut side with your plastic knife (fig. 1).

2. Press the tip of the knife gently into the potato and then rotate the knife to carve a small hole or divot (fig. 2).

3. Continue making lines and holes where you want them to be. It's fine if some of the potoato edges come off when you are carving.

4. Press the potato onto the paper towel to absorb some of the juices. Carve some more designs in the other potatoes.

5. Stack several sheets of newspaper for a padded surface, and then place your paper on top of the newspapers.

6. Press your potato on an ink pad (fig. 3); press firmly. Then press the potato onto the paper where you desire (fig. 4).

7. Continue printing with all the potatoes and ink pads.

What's the Rub?

Think First: Rub your fingers over the texture plates and feel the bumps. Look around the room for other bumpy textures: window screens, wooden floors, brick walls, and grates on a radiator are a few examples. If you don't have access to texture plates, sneaker soles, combs, coins, keys, and the like will do just fine. Become a texture detective and seek out new bumpy textures for your art prints.

Tip: This lesson adapts well to very young children. Use the larger size oil pastels whenever possible as they make a mark easily without too much pressure.

- white drawing paper
- texture plates
- unwrapped crayons or oil pastels

optional:

- watercolors, brushes, newspaper, and water
- other textural objects

Go Further

Make complete prints or artworks by rubbing found objects that create the lines and shapes desired. For example, make a house with windows and doors by rubbing objects that have squares and rectangles.

Let's Go!

Fig. 1: *Place paper over the texture plate.*

Fig. 2: *Rub color on the paper.*

1. Place your paper over the texture plate or object (fig. 1).
2. Choose a color and hold it on its side to rub on the paper (fig. 2).

Fig. 3: Layer some colors.

Fig. 4: *Fill in with watercolor.*

3. Add new colors by layering one color over the other or next to one another (fig. 3).
4. Use as many colors as you like, overlapping and making new colors as you go.
5. You can fill in the white background with watercolor paints to make your textures really stand out (fig. 4)!
6. Let the artwork dry. Now feel the paper. It is still smooth, but now has visual texture—texture you can see, but cannot feel.

Meet the Artist: Erik Boettcher

Erik Boettcher is a New Hampshire artist who prints with found objects and assembles them into art works. His work embraces vintage machines, old metal parts, and many icons from the mid-twentieth century. Find more of Erik's work at www.artstreamstudios.com.

Garden State by Erik Boettcher

Materials

- cover stock or other heavy paper
- watercolor brush
- watercolor paint
- Plexiglas plate
- newspaper
- wash water

Tip

This lesson is perfect for even the youngest child.

Go Further

- When your print is dry, you can draw with pencil, oil pastel, or permanent marker to add details if you choose.
- Add some lively background music to this lesson and watch the paint dance across the plate.

Think First: It's fun to paint on a slippery surface—one that doesn't exactly hold the shape of what you expected. Embrace the rainbows, the swirls, and the dots for this lesson as they are natural patterns which will occur on the plate. Keep in mind that this is a loose exercise in painting and printmaking. Details are not important and can be added later if desired.

Let's Go!

Fig. 1: *Load the paint into the brush.*

Fig. 2: *Paint the plate.*

1. Put a piece of the printing paper underneath the Plexiglas plate as a guide to the actual area of your painting.

2. Starting with a very wet brush, load your brush with color (fig. 1).

3. Begin painting the plate as you like.

4. Choose more colors and continue painting until your printing plate is full (fig. 2).

5. Take your printing paper and line it up with the guide paper (fig. 3).

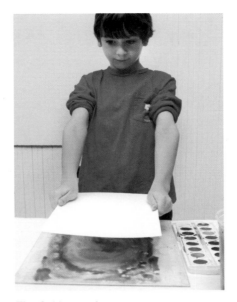

Fig. 3: *Line up the paper.*

Fig. 4: *Rub the printing paper.*

6. Lower it carefully onto the plate and rub the back of the paper gently with your hands (fig. 4).

7. Peel off your print and let it dry (fig. 5).

Fig. 5: *Peel off the print.*

Meet the Author: Susan Schwake

"This monotype was made as a response to my friend Jennifer Caswell's poem by the same name. It was a spontaneous color play printmaking session with a Plexiglas plate and a coffee filter. When it was dry I made the clear overlay with the sunglasses. Life through pink sunglasses!"

Pink Sunglasses by Susan Schwake

Glue Prints

- white or clear glue (such as Elmer's)
- mat board
- water-based block printing ink
- brayer
- newspaper
- foam tray
- pencil

Think First: Glue prints can be simple or as detailed as you want to make them. They are the perfect art lesson for even the very young. Using a glue bottle to drip or trace around your printing plate is a lot of fun. I like to use clear Elmer's glue because you can see your pencil lines, it is nice and thick coming out of the bottle, and washes up quickly. Decide if you want to draw your idea first, or not draw at all before adding the glue!

Tip

For very young children, forego the pencil stage, and let them drip and drop the glue from the bottle right onto the mat board. Beware of too much glue—encourage making dots.

Go Further

- Try making two plates to make a two-colored print. Print one color, let it dry overnight, and then print the second color.
- Try printing on colored paper or try colorful inks on white paper.

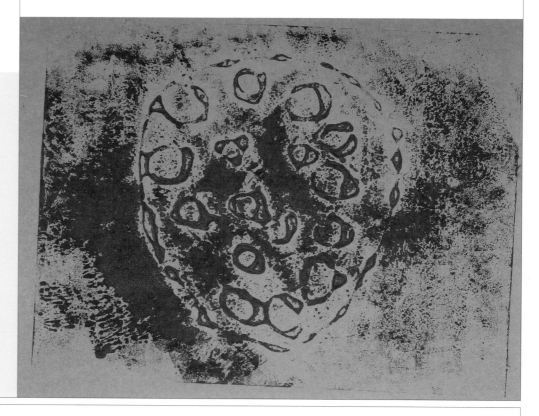

Let's Go!

Fig. 1: *Draw with glue on the board.*

1. Draw your idea onto the mat board if you desire.

2. Begin drawing your subject matter with glue (fig. 1).

3. Continue until your idea and everything you want to show in your print is outlined with glue. This will be your printing plate.

4. Let the glue dry overnight. The next day you will be ready to print!

5. Use the brayer to roll out some ink on a foam tray (fig. 2). (See "Unit 1.")

6. Roll the ink over the dried glue, making sure all of your glue lines are covered (fig. 3).

7. Place the paper over the plate. Rub the paper with your flat hand, using firm pressure, and feeling all the lines with your fingertips (fig. 4).

8. Peel off your print and let it dry overnight.

Fig. 2: *Prepare the ink.*

Fig. 3: *Ink over the dried glue.*

Fig. 4: *Rub the paper.*

Meet the Artist: John Terry Downs

John Terry Downs is a printmaker who lives in New Hampshire. He is a recently retired professor of art from Plymouth State University and an active member of the Ogunquit Art Association and Boston Printmakers Society. His work in printmaking ranges from realistic intaglios to abstract monotypes as shown here.

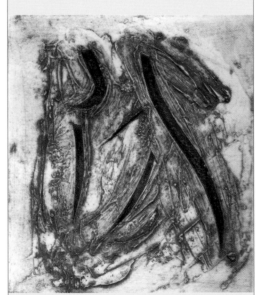

Walker by John Terry Downs

Lace Prints

- assorted laces
- cover stock
- water-based block printing ink
- brayer
- newspaper
- foam tray
- Plexiglas sheet

Think First: Lace, edging, sequin waste, or anything flat with holes can make beautiful prints. Experiment with paper doilies or plastic ones if you can find them. Hunting around the house or a yard sale is a big part of the fun! Water-based inks wash out of most items, though some ink colors can stain.

Tip

This is a fun printmaking exercise for even the very young. Just monitor how much ink they use.

Go Further

- Try using colorful inks on colored paper.
- Try white ink on a dark colored paper for a real lace effect!

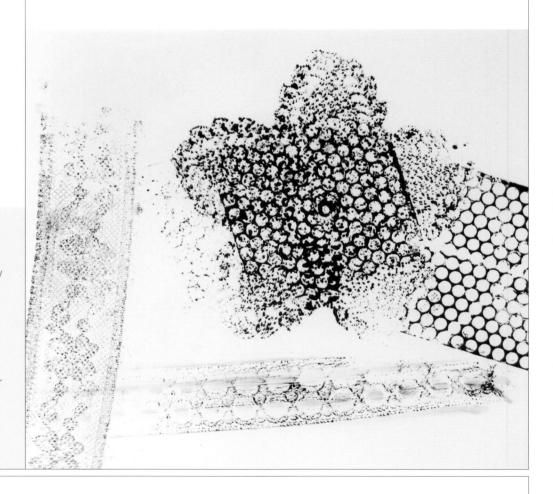

Let's Go!

Fig. 1: *Ink the lace.*

Fig. 2: *Print with the lace.*

Fig. 3: *Expose the print.*

Fig. 4: *Continue printing.*

1. Choose the first lace to be printed and place it on the Plexiglas or foam tray.

2. Roll out your ink until it is smooth and then roll it over the lace (fig. 1).

3. Stack a few layers of newspaper under your printing paper for cushion.

4. Place the lace with the ink side down on your paper. Press firmly with an open hand (fig. 2). If the lace has a lot of holes, you can cover it with a second piece of paper and press firmly.

5. Peel off the lace (fig. 3).

6. Continue inking different laces (fig. 4), and printing all over your paper until you are satisfied.

7. Let your print dry overnight.

Meet the Artist: Heather Smith Jones

Heather Smith Jones is an artist working in mixed media on paper, painting, photography, and printmaking. Smith Jones teaches in the Arts-Based Preschool at the Lawrence Arts Center and has taught art at all age levels. She is the author of *Water Paper Paint, Exploring Creativity with Watercolor and Mixed Media.* Learn more about Heather at www.heathersmithjones.com.

Grandma's Letters by Heather Smith Jones

Balloon Prints

Think First: This is a fun Lab for the very young child, but older children (and adults) will enjoy it just as much. The thought process is all about color here—which colors do you combine to make new colors, tints, or shades? Starting with three colors is recommended and having a few balloons and trays ready to continue is a good idea. It's bouncy, colorful fun, and you won't want to stop at just one print. So dispense your first three colors, blow up your balloon, and get ready to go!

- tempera or acrylic paint
- white cover stock
- newspaper
- foam tray
- balloon, partially inflated

Tip

This is a playful activity for the littles. Monitor the amount of paint they use by starting with only a coin-size amount.

Go Further

These textural prints are beautiful just as they are, or they can be used as backgrounds for collage, paintings, or other mixed-media works. Give the child the options and let them decide.

Let's Go!

Fig. 1: *Dip into the paint.*

Fig. 2: *Print the first color.*

1. Dip your balloon into the first paint color (fig. 1).
2. Press the balloon on the paper to make a print (fig. 2).
3. Pull the balloon up to see the mark, and then bounce it on the paper.
4. Continue to bounce the balloon without getting more paint (fig. 3).
5. Check the bottom of the balloon to see if your paint is mostly gone.

Fig. 3: *Continue bouncing.*

Fig. 4: Use the second color.

6. Dip into your second color and bounce some more (fig. 4).
7. Bounce over the marks you already made, and then dip into the third color when you run out of paint.
8. Continue until you are satisfied with the print.
9. Let dry, and try another print with three new colors.

Meet the Artist: Anne O. Smith

Anne O. Smith lives in Strafford, New Hampshire, and is an artist whose work is whimsical, abstract, and often includes collage work. She is a member of the New Hampshire Art Association and exhibits frequently. More of her work can be found at www.artstreamstudios.com.

Heard it Through the Grapevine by Anne O. Smith

Let's Print Circles & Lines

Materials

- black water-based block printing ink
- white cover stock
- foam trays
- assortment of found items: rulers, paper tubes, bubble wrap, and recycled objects
- brayer
- newspaper

Go Further

- Try colored papers or colored inks for different effects.
- Making these prints with shaped objects help children recognize the basic shapes found all around them.

Think First: Did you know you could print lines and circles using things around your home? See if you can find some straight lines on rulers, wood, scrapers, and toys. Look for circles on paper tubes, plastic lids, tennis balls, and bubble wrap. There are so many objects you can use, but remember to ask permission before printing with them!

Tip: For the smallest child, make sure that they have tiny objects to print with. Little hands can't hold big objects easily. Be sure to supervise so the small objects don't go in their mouths.

Let's Go!

Fig. 1: Ink the object.

Fig. 2: Print lines on the paper.

1. Lay out all of your objects in front of you. Get your ink ready by rolling it out on the foam tray using the brayer.
2. Roll the ink onto the first object to print (fig. 1).

Fig. 3: Print with more objects.

3. Press the object onto the paper (fig. 2).
4. Continue inking up different objects and printing them (fig. 3).
5. See what your objects could make if you used them all together (fig. 4). A house? A fence? A solar system?
6. Try all of your different objects and make a lot of prints.

Meet the Artist: Edibeth Farrington

Edibeth says, "Making marks, pulling images, and being creative is all about pushing out that which is within me—past stories and memories. I like placing hints and little gems of reality, but primarily I want my work to be relished, thought about, and to make a connection with the viewer, and hopefully for them to have an 'ah-ha' moment."

Fig. 4: Observe the possibilities.

Sad Proof by Edibeth Farrington

Sculpture

PAPER IS A STAPLE IN THE ART STUDIO, and most art budgets can include paper as a material for creating artwork. This Unit explores using paper as the medium for a substrate, as a structure, and for color, texture, and value. We will create collages, masks, monsters, and our own textured papers from recycled maps, magazines, and other printed materials. Paper can be used in art forms in endless ways. These Labs are springboards to other places, in which you can experiment with paper further and transform it with other media.

LAB 31 Tinfoil Fun

Materials

- block of wood or wooden cigar box for base
- tinfoil
- hot glue gun and glue sticks (to be used by adult)

Think First: Stand up and make a pose with your arms and legs—freeze in that pose! Have someone else make a pose and look at how long their arms and legs are. When modeling with tinfoil, remember not to squeeze it too tight at the beginning. The foil is easier to adjust when it's not compressed too tightly.

Tip: For the littlest children, this lesson's subject matter will be a little beyond their grasp. Do let them try to shape the foil into their own ideas. Modeling with foil is a wonderful opportunity for very young children to learn about three-dimensional forms. Stand back and let their ideas blossom!

Meet the Artist: Adam Pearson

Adam is a Barrington, New Hampshire, sculptor and craftsman. Currently, he works at UNH as the art department technician where he coordinates safety protocol, machine maintenance, and material usage in the sculpture, ceramics, welding, and casting areas. See Adam's metal sculptures at: www.pearsonsculpture.com.

Tree by Adam Pearson

Let's Go!

Fig. 1: *Gather the tinfoil.*

Fig. 3: *Add the head.*

Fig. 5: *Form the body.*

Fig. 2: *Cross the sticks.*

Fig. 4: *Create the arms.*

Fig. 6: *Make the feet.*

1. Rip off five sheets of tinfoil about 12 to 15 inches (30.5 to 38 cm) long; a little longer or shorter doesn't make any difference.

2. Have the child gather each sheet of foil gently—not tightly—and make loose sticks: two for the legs, two for the arms, and one for the head/neck/body section (fig. 1).

3. Cross two of the sticks at one end and twist them lightly together (fig. 2).

4. Add the head/neck/body stick by folding it in half from the back over the front of the twisted part of the legs (fig. 3); squeeze lightly to hold.

5. Put the remaining sticks on the table perpendicular to the body. Fold them across the body to add weight to the body and to create the arms (fig. 4). Squeeze a bit tighter this time.

6. Mold the different body parts as you wish, squeezing a little tighter now to create the form (fig. 5). The head, hands, and feet can be shaped at this time (fig. 6).

7. Bend your silver person into the pose you desire, and have an adult hot glue the feet to your base.

Go Further
- Try making two silver people interacting on your base.
- Make a pet for your silver person!

LAB 32 Mat Board Stacks

Materials

- mat board cut into small assorted sizes
- backing board of wood or mat board, sized to fit the assorted smaller boards
- oil pastels
- clear glue

optional:
- watercolor
- brushes and water

Think First: This will be a relief sculpture meant to either hang on the wall or sit on a table. It is built up as the artist chooses, so there is no wrong way to create it. The artist may choose to begin by trying different stacking patterns.

Tip
This lesson works well for the littlest of children as they naturally love to stack and build!

Go Further
Create a theme for the topmost panels, such as nature, animals, or colors.

Let's Go!

Fig. 1: *Draw on the mat board.*

Fig. 2: *Arrange into piles.*

Fig. 3: *Add the colorful boards.*

4. Use the glue to adhere each piece of board in your piles to one another, ending with the colorful boards on top (fig. 4). Let the piles dry overnight.

5. If you choose, add watercolor to your shapes when the glue is dry.

Fig. 4: *Glue the boards together.*

1. Choose a few of the mat board pieces to draw on. Using oil pastels, draw or color on one side of the chosen boards (fig. 1).

2. Arrange the remaining boards in little piles on top of your backing board (fig. 2).

3. Place the colorful boards on top of the piles as you desire (fig. 3).

Meet the Artist:
Judith Heller Cassell

Judith Heller Cassell is a celebrated artist and member of the Boston Printmakers Association. Her work ranges from printmaking to sculpture and sometimes mixing the two mediums together. The work shown here was created in copper, wood, and mixed media. Judith's prints are often in our artstream studio gallery at www.artstreamstudios.com.

Preservation by Judith Heller Cassell

- low-fire clay
- rib tool for clay
- water
- scoring tool
- low-fire underglaze
- low-fire clear glaze
- Masonite board or canvas
- pencil
- fruits and vegetables for reference

Think First: Lots of artists sketch fruits and vegetables for a still life, but some like to make sculptures of their favorites. Pick up some real vegetables and feel their curves and shape. This helps when it comes time to mold them with the clay. For this lesson, we will demonstrate molding a carrot. There is no limit to what you can make with clay. Try making an entire bowl of fruit with this method.

Meet the Artist: Cada Driscoll

Cada Driscoll is a New Hampshire artist who creates work in clay and mixed media. Her clay carrots are whimsical little wall sculptures that inspired this lesson. Find out more about Cada at her blog www.cadacreates.blogspot.com.

Carrots by Cada Driscoll

Let's Go!

Fig. 1: Roll the clay.

1. Begin with a small amount of wedged clay (see "Unit 1") that easily fits in your palm. Roll it into a tube shape on the board or between your hands (fig. 1).

2. Taper one end to form the carrot's pointed end. Use the pencil to poke a hole and hollow out the fatter end (fig. 2).

Let's Go! (continued)

3. Smooth out the surfaces with your finger (fig. 3).
4. Use the rib tool to create lines on the outside of the carrot (fig. 4). If you use a pointed tool, such as a pencil, to create the lines, you will create small shards of clay. Make sure you brush them off your carrot before putting it into the kiln; they become sharp after firing.
5. Roll some clay to make three "snakes" for the carrot top (fig. 5).
6. Using the scoring tool, scrape the fat end of the carrot around the hole and one end of each carrot top—dip the scoring tool in water to create muddy scoring lines (fig. 6).
7. Attach the carrot tops to the carrot at the score lines (fig. 7).
8. Smooth the connecting areas to make sure the top is secured to the carrot.
9. Let dry completely until the carrot is no longer cool to the touch. Paint with underglaze and fire. Add clear glaze if desired and fire again. (See "Unit 1.")

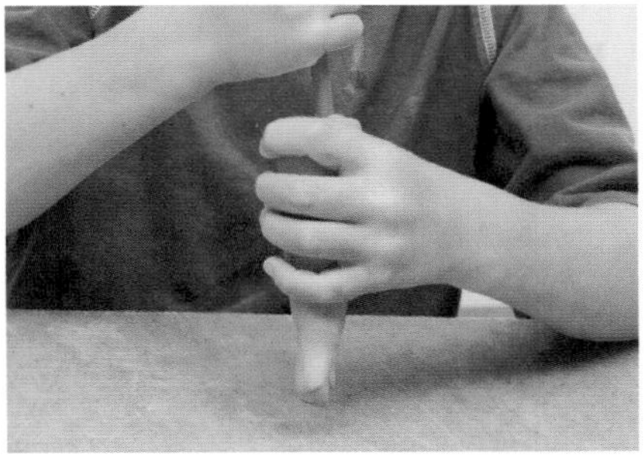

Fig. 2: *Hollow out the other end.*

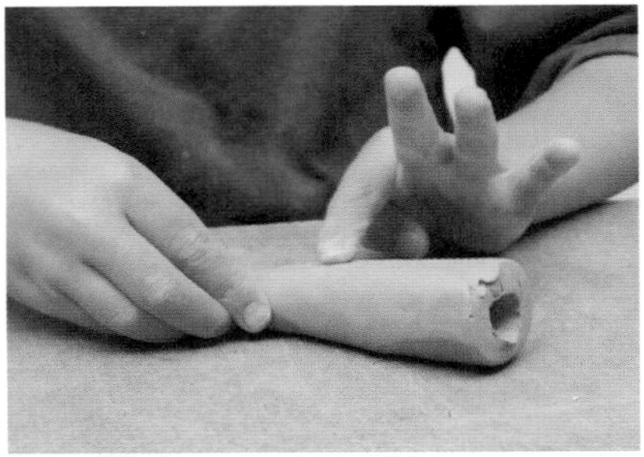

Fig. 3: *Smooth the carrot suface.*

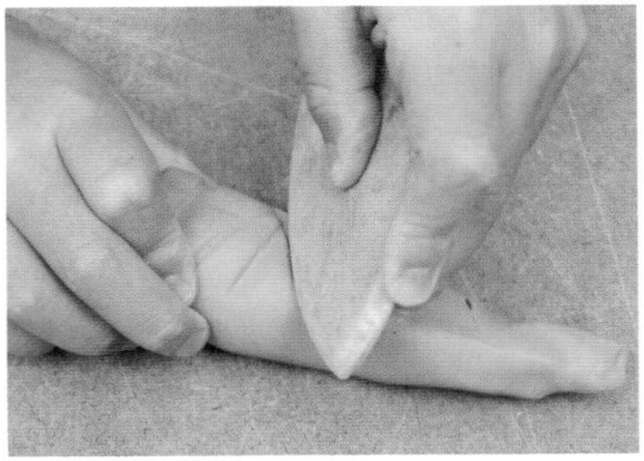

Fig. 4: *Add the lines.*

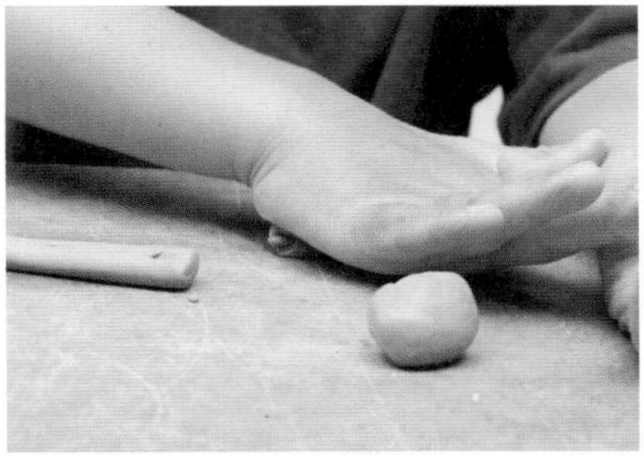

Fig. 5: *Make the tops.*

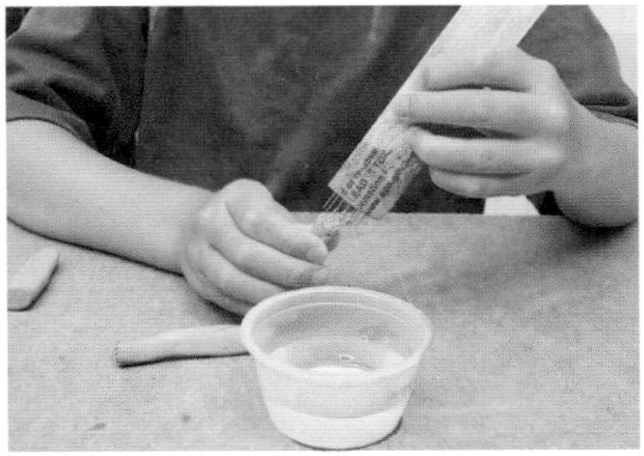

Fig. 6: *Score the contact points.*

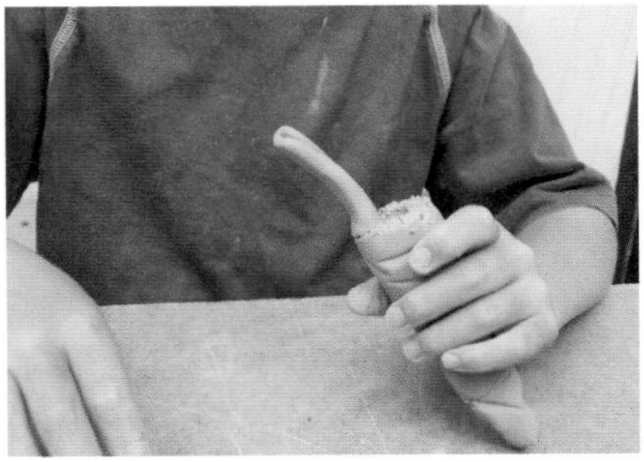

Fig. 7: *Attach the tops.*

Tube Construction

Materials

- assortment of paper tubes
- clear glue in small containers for dipping
- clear glue in bottle
- mat board for base
- acrylic paint
- scissors

Think First: Arrange a few of the tubes on your base to get a feel for size, design, and height. If you need to cut some tubes shorter, now is a good time for that. Try to get an idea of how you want them to be—you can always change your mind as you go.

Tip

This is a fun project for the littlest—just be there to help them with the glue!

Go Further

- You can use other shaped cardboard containers: small boxes, cartons, and cereal boxes to create other sculptures.
- Go big! Get a large piece of cardboard for the base and glue larger boxes for your sculpture.

Let's Go!

Fig. 1: Arrange the tubes.

Fig. 2: Dip a tube in glue.

Fig. 3: Build up your sculpture.

Fig. 4: Add extra glue.

Fig. 5: Paint your sculpture.

1. Arrange your tubes on the base as you choose (fig. 1).
2. Dip one tube into the glue (fig. 2).
3. Continue adding the tubes by dipping each one into the glue and placing them on your base (fig. 3).
4. When you are finished, use the bottle to add extra glue around any areas that need it (fig. 4); let dry overnight.
5. Choose one or two colors to paint your sculpture (fig. 5).
6. Let dry and then hang it on the wall or display on a table!

Meet the Artist: Megan Bogonovich

"I am always delighted by a story and there are so many plots lines to follow: novels, Netflix, newspapers, podcasts, love stories, history, family drama, political antics, and gossip. These plots bring to life characters, costumes, and environments. They interact. They repeat. Coming of age and falling in love are both timeless themes. They are worthy of pop songs and they are worthy of porcelain figurines." Learn more about Megan at her website at www.meganbogonovich.com.

Figurine Collage by Megan Bogonovich

LAB 35 Masks

- mat board for backing
- tinfoil
- pencil
- clear glue
- colored tape
- paint markers

optional:

- feathers, beads, yarn, string

Think First: Masks are found in every culture all over the world. This mask will start as a mold of your face and then become whatever you would like it to be! This mask will be a decorative work to hang on the wall, not to wear.

Tip

Small children may not like the feeling of the foil on their faces. Let those children start with a bowl or large doll to mold their foil over.

Go Further

Make a mask of your favorite cartoon character.

Let's Go!

Fig. 1: *Mold your foil.*

1. Tear off a piece of tinfoil larger than your face. Place the foil over your face and mold it (fig. 1).

2. Place the foil shape on the backing board. Cut off the excess at the sides (fig. 2).

3. Using a pencil and with one hand under the mask, poke holes for the eyes (fig. 3).

4. Add colorful tape and use paint markers to add color and emotion to the mask. You could also add additional embellishments (fig. 4).

5. Apply clear glue along the sides to glue the mask to the backing; let dry completely. Hang your artwork on the wall!

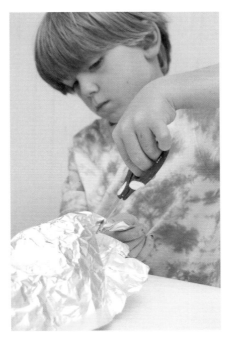

Fig. 2: *Trim the edges.*

Fig. 3: *Poke eye holes.*

Fig. 4: *Add the color.*

Artistic Inspiration: Masks of the World

These Balinese dance masks are used for a specific dance ritual performed in Indonesia. There are many books, websites, and films where masks are featured. They are used for rituals, parades, traditions, dance, theater, and many other purposes. Find as many as you can and make more of your own!

Balinese Dance Masks

Paper Vases

- three paper or plastic cups
- white flour
- water
- bowl
- newspaper torn into strips and small pieces
- masking tape
- colored tissue paper
- sand

optional:

- acrylic sealer and paint

Think First: This vase will be used for decoration and to hold paper or silk flowers, not to hold water. It can also hold beautiful dried flowers or small branches from your yard. Think about how you might like to decorate this simple, elegant shape.

Tip: For younger children, making the vase with smaller plastic cups can be less daunting.

Go Further

- Make a taller vase by adding two more cups!
- Paint the vase with acrylic paint instead of applying tissue paper— wait until the paper mâché is dry before painting.

Let's Go!

Fig. 1: Tape the third cup.

Fig. 2: Begin the paper mâché process.

1. Begin by adding sand to the bottom cup. Tape the second cup to the bottom cup with masking tape. Securely tape the bottom of the second cup to the bottom of the third (fig. 1).

2. Mix the flour and water together for the paper mâché goo (see "Unit 1"). Dip the newspaper strips and pieces one at a time into the goo (fig. 2). Smooth the strips and pieces onto the bottom half.

3. Continue applying the newspaper until you reach the top (fig. 3). Cover the inside too!

Fig. 3: Finish the paper mâché layers.

Fig. 4: Add the colored tissue.

4. Add two layers of paper mâché over the cups.

5. While the second layer is still wet, begin applying the tissue paper to the vase using the goo on your fingers (fig. 4).

Artistic Inspiration: Incan Polychrome Jar

The Incans created this jar sometime between 1471 and 1493. The Incans created many jars, vases, and containers among their many other creative achievements. This jar has a wonderful shape and is part of the collection at the Indianapolis Children's Museum, in Indianapolis, Indiana.

Incan Polychrome Jar

6. Add tissue paper to cover the vase completely and let dry. Add watercolors over the dry tissue if a richer color is desired. Paint a coating of acrylic sealer on the vase to make it shiny.

Royal Crowns

- white heavyweight paper 12" × 24" (30.5 × 61 cm)
- oil pastels
- watercolor paints
- watercolor brushes
- wash water
- newspaper
- glitter
- clear glue
- shallow box

Think First: Everyone wants to be royalty sometimes: either king or queen, or at least a prince or princess! So why not crown yourself? There are many types of crowns from different countries. Take a trip to your local library or go online to find inspiration for your crown. Think about the colors you would like to use and the shape of the crown's profile, or upper edge. You can make a sketch or two of what your crown will look like before you begin.

Tip

These crowns are popular with littler children too. They may need extra help with the scissors, but it's a great way to practice cutting too!

Go Further

Make a crown for a special occasion— a birthday, holiday, or to cheer someone up if they are sick.

Let's Go!

Fig. 1: *Cut along the line.*

Fig. 3: *Add the watercolor.*

Fig. 5: *Sprinkle on the glitter.*

Fig. 2: *Color shapes with oil pastel.*

Fig. 4: *Draw with the glue.*

1. Draw the crown's upper edge along the paper's long edge.

2. Cut out, or have an adult help you cut along the line you drew (fig. 1).

3. Use oil pastels to color shapes for your decorations and gems (fig. 2). Remember you will also use glitter and watercolors to decorate your crown.

4. Paint watercolors where the white paper is still visible (fig. 3). Use a wet brush for even coverage; let the paint dry.

5. Use the clear glue to make lines or shapes where you want to sprinkle glitter (fig. 4).

6. Put your crown in the box to help contain the glitter; sprinkle on the sparkle (fig. 5).

7. Let the glue dry completely. Fit the crown around your head and tape in place. Go rule your world!

Artistic Inspiration: Crown of King Christian IV of Denmark

The crown of King Christian IV of Denmark, is currently located in Rosenborg Castle, Copenhagen. It is one of the many crowns you can learn about at your local library or online. They represent royalty and a monarch-type government. They are also beautiful sculptures to wear! What kind of crown would you like to wear?

The crown of King Christian IV of Denmark

38 Mat Board Mobiles

- three pieces of mat board, graduated in size
- oil pastels
- watercolor paints
- thin wire, string, or ribbon
- newspaper
- hole punch
- wash water

Tip

Small children may choose to just scribble with wild abandon on the mat board. This works well too!

Artistic Inspiration: Alexander Calder

Alexander Calder was the father of wire sculpture and mobiles. His work in mobiles is known around the world. For more information on Alexander Calder you can look at www.calder.org.

Think First: This Lab is adaptable to different subject matter. We chose a landscape for ours, dividing the three boards into land, water, and sky. You could try an abstract subject matter and enjoy a scribblefest on each board. Portraits are fun—dividing up a face into eyes, nose and mouth or head, torso, and legs. Still life exploration could be endless, too. Just decide on a subject to begin! Then try it over and over again.

Note: An adult should use a hole punch to make the holes at the top and bottom of each board before beginning. The holes can be made easily with a three-hole punch using just one of the holes (fig. 1). A hand punch is more difficult.

Let's Go!

Fig. 1: *Use the three-hole punch.*

Fig. 3: *Draw on all the boards.*

Fig. 2: *Begin the first board.*

1. Begin with the oil pastels, drawing your sky on the smallest or largest board (fig. 2). Think about what the weather is like: cloudy, rainy, or sunny?

2. Flip the board over and make the same or a different sky on the other side.

3. Proceed with the second and third boards (fig. 3).

4. When both sides are finished with the oil pastels, you can proceed to the watercolor. Paint over the oil pastels and fill in the spaces with paint (fig. 4).

5. When dry, flip the boards over and paint the other side.

6. When everything is dry, string them together using thin wire, ribbon, string, or a combination of these items. Hang your mobile up where everyone can see it!

Fig. 4: *Use the watercolors.*

Go Further

• Try making a family tree from this project. Start with the grandparents on the top board, the parents on the middle board, and the children on the bottom board.

• Experiment with using more than three boards in your mobile.

Fairy & Toad Houses

- low-fire clay
- low-fire underglaze
- low-fire clear glaze
- texture-making objects
- clay knife or plastic knife
- Masonite board or canvas to work on

Meet the Artist: Jane Kaufmann

Jane is a beloved and honored ceramic artist from Durham, NH. She says about her work, "I feel it is the artist's duty to address what is going on in the world. I think the artist should do this so the work can be understood by everyone. I believe artists can help save the world." www.janekaufmann.com.

Village Orb by Jane Kaufman

Think First: These tiny houses are made to sit in a special spot outside in good weather, be it under a tree, on a porch, in a garden, or on a stoop. They are made with your own hands so the fairy (or toad) knows you are sincerely interested in their well-being. They are tiny—just the right size for one occupant. Decide the colors and textures you might like to have on the outside of the house to make your fairy (or toad) the happiest!

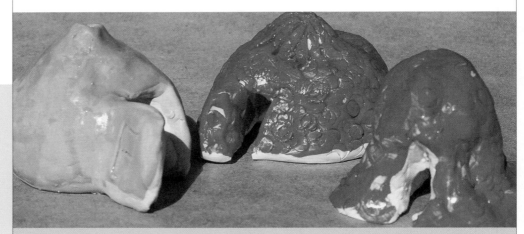

Let's Go!

Fig. 1: Make the hole.

1. Pinch off a small ball of clay to fit in your palm. Wedge it (see "Unit 1") if it has been used before to eliminate air bubbles. Roll the clay into a ball.

2. Hold the ball of clay in the hand that you do not write with. Push the thumb of your other hand into the ball almost to the bottom, but not through it (fig. 1).

Let's Go! (continued)

3. Leave your thumb in your ball of clay and then begin pinching around the opening. Take your time and use small pinching motions between your thumb and first two (or three) fingers around the ball (fig. 2).

4. Continue pinching around the ball of clay, moving in a spiral motion toward the top (fig. 3). Try to keep the opening only as big as your thumb for as long as you can.

5. When you get to the top of the ball, take it off of your thumb and spread the opening as far as you wish for the base of the house (fig. 4).

6. When the house is the size you want, put it on the table and cut a door with the knife. You can mark the door first with a pencil. Leave one side of the door uncut if you want your house to have an "open door" (fig. 5).

7. Add texture to the outside or draw details with a pencil (fig. 6) and remove any little balls of clay that the pencil creates.

8. Let your house dry until it is no longer cool to the touch; paint with underglaze and fire (fig. 7).

9. Coat with clear glaze if desired and then fire again.

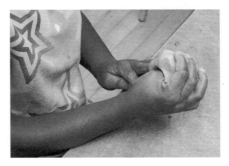

Fig. 2: Pinch around the opening.

Fig. 3: Spiral up the ball of clay.

Fig. 4: Open up the base.

Fig. 5: Cut a door.

Fig. 6: Add details.

Fig. 7: Paint on the underglaze.

Personal Piñatas

- newspaper
- flour and water mixed (see "Unit 1.")
- small balloon
- tall quart-size recycled container
- masking tape
- tempera or acrylic paint
- colored paper or streamers
- glue
- glitter

Go Further

Try a making a more complicated shape by taping on balls, cones, or tubes of newspaper to your balloon shape.

Think First: This Lab is about making a toy—one that can be broken or used as a decoration. Piñatas are familiar items in Mexico where they have been made and used for centuries. Piñatas come in all shapes and sizes with colorful outsides and candy and little toys on the inside. Ours will be a small personal-size piñata, which can be hung in a child's room or elsewhere for everyone to enjoy. Think about the colors and the designs you might like to put on the outside of yours!

Tip: This process can be fun for those who enjoy the goo. Be aware that very small children will do best with your hands working along with theirs.

Artistic Inspiration: Piñatas of the World!

There are so many different countries using piñatas as a toy or game—in Mexico there is a statue of a monk hitting a piñata. Enjoy reading about piñatas at your local library or online.

A nine-pointed star piñata

Let's Go!

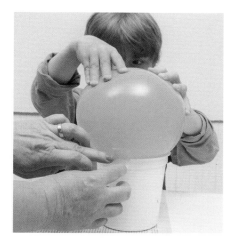

Fig. 1: Tape the balloon to the container.

Fig. 2: Scrape off excess goo.

Fig. 4: Pop the balloon.

Fig. 3: Smooth on the strips.

Fig. 5: Cut the top opening.

Fig. 6: Add streamers.

1. Inflate the balloon and tape it to the tall quart-size container for stability (fig. 1). Tear the newspaper into strips no larger than 2 × 4 inches (5 × 10 cm).

2. Dip the strips into the flour and water mixture and scrape the excess off with two fingers (fig. 2).

3. Smooth the strips onto the balloon. Continue until the whole balloon is covered with two layers (fig. 3); let dry completely.

4. Pop the balloon (fig. 4) and pull it out. If the balloon is stuck, you can trim the paper mâché.

5. Cut the opening to the size you would like (fig. 5). This artist chose to open it up so he could use the piñata as a candy holder. Paint with the colors and designs you have chosen. It's nice to paint the inside too.

6. Cut strips of paper or use rolled crepe paper for streamers to hang from the bottom. Attach the streamers with clear glue (fig. 6).

7. Punch three holes around the opening for a string to hang your piñata.

Paper Mâché Minis

Materials

Materials

- newspaper
- flour and water mixed (See "Unit 1.")
- white paper towels
- colored tissue paper
- waxed paper

Think First: With paper mâché, you can make very large and very small sculptures. For this Lab, we will make a tiny fish. There is no limit to the kinds of tiny sculptures you can create, and animals are a good place to start. This sculpture works best with subject matter that does not have long extensions or extra parts that hang off the main piece. Keep it simple, and it will be fun. What will you make?

Tip: This lesson is fun for the smallest child as they can make simple-shaped objects right in their hand.

Go Further

- Try making a whole zoo filled with tiny animals.
- Tie several fish to a dowel for a fish mobile!

Let's Go!

Fig. 1: *Squeeze excess goo from the paper towel.*

Fig. 2: *Shape the fish.*

Fig. 3: *Add another paper towel.*

Fig. 4: *Add color with tissue paper.*

1. Mix up the paper mâché goo.
2. Dip the paper towel into the bowl of paper mâché goo. Squish it together and squeeze the excess goo back into the bowl (fig. 1).
3. Shape with your hands to the desired subject you have chosen (fig. 2).
4. Add another paper towel in the same fashion, keeping everything very wet and compacted (fig. 3).

5. Continue molding the wet paper until you are satisfied with your sculpture.
6. Smooth small pieces of dry tissue paper over the wet object to add color. The wet goo will hold the tissue paper in place (fig. 4).
7. Dry completely and hang up your sculpture with string or glue it to a base.

Meet the Artist: Carol Roll

Carol Roll is an artist from Florida who makes whimsical folk art from paper mâché. The sculpture titled *Pout* has a paper mâché head with delicate features. More of her work can be found at her website at www.nostalgicfolkart.com.

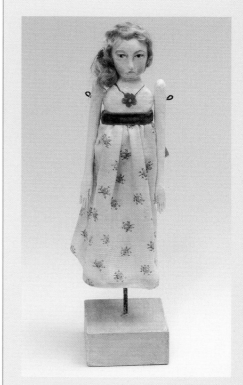

Pout by Carol Roll

Mixed Media

LITTLE CHILDREN LOVE THE PROCESSES involved in mixed media. Layer upon layer of materials involving glue, fabric, sand, salt, and more, more, more is just pure fun for the small child. The challenge is to let the process unfold for the child in a nonoverwhelming manner. Presenting materials one at a time is often a good method for keeping the process fun—just where it belongs. Sometimes we will start the process with glue and paper and other times with an oil pastel and pencil. These Labs can be used over and over again with different results each time. Just by changing the paper color or subject matter, the lesson will spark a different creative note. Dive into mixed media!

LAB 42 Fabric Collage

Materials

Think First: Collages are works of art made up of paper, or in this case fabric. Using fabric to make the subjects in your work can be challenging. If you want to work with scissors, you can try cutting the smaller pieces into the shapes you want, or ask an adult to help. It's fun to try and make something from precut shapes too. Most of all—have fun using patterned, fuzzy, thin, or thick fabric as your media.

- small wooden board
- paint markers
- scrap fabrics cut into small shapes
- clear glue
- glue brush
- Plexiglas plate

Tip

The younger child will need everthing ready to sort, arrange, and glue.

Go Further

Try making a picture inspired by a quilt made by Jan Burgwinkle or Gee's Bend quilts. Go to your library to learn more about Gee's Bend quilts!

Meet the Artist: Jan Burgwinkle

Jan Burgwinkle started sewing when she was 10 years old and has been playing with fabric ever since. A former kindergarten through twelfth grade art teacher, she has been making quilts for over thirty years. Mixing unexpected colors and patterns is her favorite part of designing quilts. Visit her at bemused.typepad.com.

Scrap Bag by Jan Burgwinkle

Let's Go!

Fig. 1: Arrange the pieces.

1. Begin by admiring your piles of fabric. We sorted ours into solid colors and patterns.

2. Arrange the fabric pieces onto the wooden board however you like (fig. 1).

3. Place the fabric on the Plexiglas plate and brush the glue onto the back side of the fabric (fig. 2). Brush the glue completely off the edges.

4. Place the fabric right side up on the wood and press firmly with your fingertips (fig. 3).

5. Continue until your fabric is all glued down (fig. 4).

6. If you desire, finish the collage by using a paint marker on the wood that is still showing (fig. 5).

Fig. 2: Brush the fabric with glue.

Fig. 3: Press down on the fabric.

Fig. 4: Add more fabric.

Fig. 5: Finish with a paint marker.

Sewing Cards

Materials

- small square of cardstock
- crayons or oil pastels
- black permanent marker
- hole punch or screw punch
- yarn
- masking tape

Think First: Sewing or lacing cards are as much fun to make as they are to play with. Most hole punches don't have a long reach. A Japanese screw punch, which is a book-binding tool, can easily make a hole anywhere. We kept our holes closer to the edge so we could reach the locations with a hand punch.

Tip

Any design can be made into a sewing card. An adult should help punch the holes, but the children should be able to do the rest!

Go Further

You can laminate your sewing cards to extend their life!

Let's Go!

Fig. 1: Draw the design.

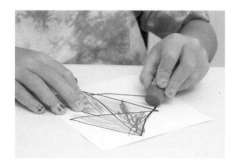

Fig. 2: Add color.

Fig. 3: Tape for the yarn ends

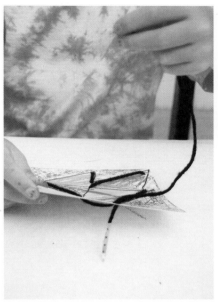

Fig. 4: Lace yarn through the holes.

1. Draw your design with a black marker (fig. 1).
2. Add color with your oil pastels or crayons (fig. 2).
3. Punch the holes where you want the lacing to go through.
4. Wrap a bit of tape around the ends of your yarn to make it easier to push through the holes (fig. 3).
5. Lace up your design (fig. 4).

Artistic Inspiration:
Vintage Sewing Cards

Sewing cards or lacing cards have been around forever in some form. Even today they are still made as toys for young children to play with. It's fun to make your own toys, and it is also rewarding to make something for a sister, brother, or friend to play with. If you prefer, you can use shoelaces instead of the yarn for your lacing.

Torn Paper Collage

Materials

- cardstock
- assortment of colored papers
- glue stick
- still life objects for reference, if desired

Think First: Tearing up paper is a fun way to get into a creative mood. It is the finger painting of collage art! Set up a simple still life with fruit and/or flowers. Have the kids hold the objects and get a feeling for their shapes before you begin the tearing.

Tip

Having a small open box of medium-size papers helps things get started. Large pieces of paper are harder to begin tearing for little hands.

Go Further

- Try using patterned papers for this project—they can be found everywhere: recycled safety envelopes with pretty patterns inside, wallpaper samples, and magazines.
- Use simple shapes as your subject matter—fill in a square, circle, or triangle for the youngest child or more timid artist.

Let's Go!

Fig. 1: Tear up the colored paper.

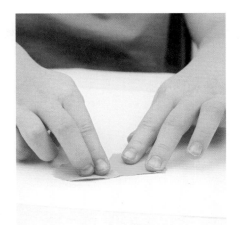

Fig. 2: Arrange the colored paper.

Fig. 3: Add glue to the paper.

1. Choose your colored papers for your objects and begin tearing them into small pieces (fig. 1). Each piece can be the shape of the object, or use a few smaller pieces to shape your subject matter.

2. Continue tearing and placing the papers on the background paper to arrange them into your composition (fig. 2).

3. When you are satisfied with the placement of the colored paper bits, start gluing them down using the method outlined in "Gluing, Tearing & Cutting Paper" on page 20 (fig. 3).

4. When everything is glued down, you can check for loose corners and reglue them.

5. Remember to press all the pieces down with your fingertips (fig. 4).

Fig. 4: Use your fingertips.

Meet the Artist: Henri Matisse

Henri Matisse was a French artist who in 1941 began making paper cutout art. His art is known around the world. For more information on Matisse and his life, visit www.henri-matissse.net.

Wild Weavings

Materials

- small piece of cardboard
- assorted yarns
- assortment of feathers, fabrics, and trims
- masking tape
- scissors

Meet the Artist: Francine Kontos

Francine Kontos is a New Hampshire weaver, ceramicist, and photographer. She also is an art teacher and inspires her students on a daily basis.

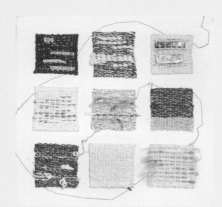

Self-Portrait Weaving by Francine Kontos

Think First: It's fun to weave with a variety of materials. You just go under and over, and you can get pretty free with your weaving art! Sort the items you wish to use so you know where everything is. Have an adult make the cuts around the edge of the cardboard with large scissors.

Tip: Small children can accomplish this weaving project with a little help at the beginning. Show them how to pull the yarn snugly for the warp threads and the under-over process will come almost naturally.

Go Further

Try making seasonal wild weavings by using colors or objects which represent the season to you.

Let's Go!

Fig. 1: *Cardboard with slits*

Fig. 2: *Start wrapping the warp yarns.*

Fig. 3: *Continue warping the loom.*

Fig. 4: *End the warp yarn on the back.*

Fig. 5: *Weave under and over.*

Fig. 6: *Add more items.*

1. Have the adult make random ½ inch (1.3 cm) long slits around the edges of the cardboard to create your loom (fig. 1).

2. Choose one color of yarn for your warp. The warp is the yarn that is held in tension on the frame of the loom (cardboard). The weft yarns are woven under and over the warp yarns.

3. Starting on the back side of the cardboard, tape your yarn down and then pull it through a slit along one edge (fig. 2)—begin anywhere.

4. Wind your yarn from the slit across the cardboard to a slit on another side of the loom. Wrap the yarn around the back and come through another slit on a different side (fig. 3)—keep it tight. The yarn can be wrapped in any way!

5. When all the slits have yarn wrapped through them, end on the back side of the cardboard, and tape down the end of the yarn (fig. 4).

6. Begin weaving with the materials you have gathered. Start under one piece of yarn, and then weave over the next. Continue weaving over the warp yarns with this under-over pattern until you are satisfied (fig. 5).

7. Keep going! Add as many items as you wish, weaving them under and over (fig. 6). More is more with this project.

Black & White & Red

Materials

- oil pastels: black, white, and red
- white drawing paper
- glue stick
- found paper: black, white, and red
- black and red permanent markers
- scissors
- pencil

Tip

For younger children, let them have the materials one at a time to keep them engaged with the process!

Go Further

Think about adding yarn, ribbon, felt, or fabric into your mix of materials! Use a thick glue to hold them down.

Think First: It's fun and a little freeing to limit yourself to three colors. In this case, we were inspired by illustrator Penelope Dullaghan's mixed-media painting, which does just that. Black, white, and red are strong colors and are often used in illustrations. Have you read a book where all the pictures were these three colors? Take a look at your library's collection and see what you find! For this Lab, we will use faces as our subject matter. Use a mirror for self portraits or make up a face like our artist did.

Let's Go!

Fig. 1: Begin with pencil.

Fig. 2: Darken lines with the black marker.

Fig. 3: Add color with paper and markers.

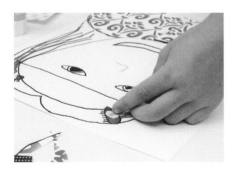

Fig. 4: Add details.

1. Begin drawing the outline of the face and the features in pencil (fig. 1).
2. Look over your materials and decide what you will use for each part of your drawing. Draw over the pencil lines with the black marker where you want darker lines (fig. 2).
3. Continue using the materials to add color to your artwork (fig. 3).
4. Add little details to finish your picture (fig. 4).

Meet the Artist: Penelope Dullaghan

Penelope Dullaghan is a freelance illustrator who has worked with numerous clients worldwide and has been recognized by *Communication Arts, Communication Arts Typography, 303 Magazine, Society of Illustrators LA,* and *Print* magazine. She also created and runs IllustrationFriday.com, a weekly creative outlet and participatory art exhibit for illustrators and artists of all skill levels. Penny lives in Raleigh, North Carolina, with husband Colin and daughter Veda. Learn more about Penelope at www.penelopedullaghan.com.

Chapped Lips by Penelope Dullaghan

Wonderful Wallpaper

Think First: Patterns are everywhere you look: in nature, in our clothing, in our bed sheets, tablecloths, and in paper. Wallpaper is famous for patterns. Look over some discarded wallpaper sample books and tear out your favorite patterns.

- cover stock or other heavy paper 12" x 18" (30.5 x 45.7 cm) or larger
- watercolor brush
- green watercolor paint or ink
- assorted wallpaper samples
- drinking straws
- assorted colors of tissue paper
- scissors
- glue stick

Tip

For young children, remind them how to use the straws. Have them blow in short bursts and take breaks between blowing!

Go Further

- Try using felt or fabric for a different looking vase.
- Make a greeting card with this method—it's always nice to get flowers!

Let's Go!

Fig. 1: Make the dots.

1. Place your paper on the table in front of you so it is the tall way (portrait). Begin dropping some green ink or watercolor in the middle of your paper (fig. 1).

2. Place the end of your straw near the dots of ink and blow the dots into stems (fig. 2). Let the ink dry.

3. Take small squares of the tissue paper and twist them into little flower shapes (fig. 3).

4. Make a dot of glue along the stem or at the end to glue on your little blooms (fig. 4).

5. Continue adding blooms.

6. Turn your wallpaper over to the back side. Line one edge of the paper up with the stems and then use a pencil to draw the shape of a vase or pot that you want your flowers to live in (fig. 5).

7. Cut out the vase, and apply the glue stick on the back side of the wallpaper, and glue down the vase onto your stems; press firmly (fig. 6).

Fig. 2: Blow the dots into stems.

Fig. 3: Make some blooms.

Fig. 4: Glue blooms to the stems.

Fig. 5: Draw the vase.

Fig. 6: Glue the vase in place.

Materials

- white cover stock
- old magazines
- glue stick
- scissors
- oil pastels
- watercolors
- wash water
- watercolor brush

Tip

For the youngest child, pick only one or two magazine cutouts to keep things simple.

Go Further

Try making up imaginary people or animals by using the head of one and the body of another. You can place them in a fantasy setting of your own design!

Think First: Choose a theme based on pictures you like in the magazines. We used *National Geographic* magazines because there are so many nature photos. Tear out the pages you like and make piles in front of you. Do you see a picture forming? Do the pages you tore out belong together? Think about narrowing down the pages you have to four or five, depending on how big the images are.

Let's Go!

Fig. 1: *Cut out pictures.*

Fig. 2: *Glue the images.*

Fig. 3: *Use oil pastels to complete the picture.*

Fig. 4: *Add watercolors.*

1. Begin cutting out your images (fig. 1).
2. Apply glue to the back of the images (fig. 2) and then glue them onto your background paper.
3. Using the oil pastels, draw around the images to create a new place for these images to live. Think about where they are, what they are doing, what the weather is like, and what time of day it is (fig. 3).
4. Use the watercolors to add more color if desired (fig. 4).

Meet the Artist: Erik Boettcher

Erik Boettcher is a mixed-media artist from New Hampshire who incorporates vintage images from magazines into his mixed-media works. Find more of Erik's work at www.artstreamstudios.com/shop.

Roller Coaster Line by Erik Boettcher

Junk Drawer Collage

- odds and ends from the master list on page 16
- mat board
- clear glue
- small plastic container for glue dipping

optional:

- pencil or oil pastels

Think First: Sort through your junk drawers, remove items that you no longer need, and put them to use here! Just think; a bubble wand can be a butterfly body, and a cork can be a smokestack. Your imagination is about to run wild—so let it!

Tips

- If you have extra heavy items, use a stronger glue, such as tacky glue. It is nontoxic and works for all ages.
- Small children should not be given small items they could choke on.

Go Further

Try making a collage about one thing using lots of different junk as our artist did.

Let's Go!

Fig. 1: *Arrange your items.*

Fig. 2: *Begin gluing.*

Fig. 3: *Glue the remaining items.*

1. Get the junk items you wish to use and lay them out in front of you. Arrange your items in a variety of shapes and ideas (fig. 1).

2. When you settle on an idea, begin dipping the junk into the glue and then press it down on the mat board (fig. 2).

3. Continue assembling your collage until you are satisfied (fig. 3). Let the glue dry overnight.

4. Add color, pencil marks, or oil pastels if desired.

Meet the Student Artist: Chloe Larochelle

Chloe Larochelle is an 18-year-old emerging artist from New Hampshire. Her work has been included in gallery exhibits around the Seacoast Region of New Hampshire. She has been making collages, jewelry, ceramic sculptures, paintings, and drawings since she was small. Recently, Chloe designed and made her prom dress—she wants to pursue fashion design in college. This junk-drawer college she made at age 6 inspired this lesson. More of her work can be found at www.etsy.com/shop/chlosephina.

H by Chloe Larochelle

Branch Weavings

Materials

Think First: Find a dry branch that has at least one or two Y shapes in it. Remove any loose bark before starting. If the branch still has leaves you can choose to keep or remove them.

Materials

- branch with at least one Y structure
- yarn, assorted colors and weights
- other found nature objects

Tip

The very young child may wish to simply wrap a branch that does not have a Y in it. Try that first, and then move on to the more involved weaving. You can tie feathers and such to a single branch too.

Go Further

Make your weaving into a wall hanging. Use the yarn and tie additional nature items hanging from down from the branch. Small pinecones would be a nice choice!

Let's Go!

Fig. 1: *Tie the yarn to the branch.*

Fig. 2: *Begin wrapping.*

Fig. 3: *Continue wrapping.*

Fig. 4: *Weave in the little Y.*

Fig. 5: *Weave in birch bark.*

1. Begin by tying, or have an adult tie, the first colored yarn on the branch at the base of the Y section (fig. 1).

2. Wrap the yarn over one arm of the Y and then under and back over the opposite arm of the Y (fig. 2).

3. Continue with this pattern or any wrapping method you desire (fig. 3). There is no wrong way to do this!

4. If you wish to change colors, just tie a new color to the yarn with a square knot. An adult can help you with this if you would like.

5. Continue wrapping as far up the branch as desired. You can also wrap yarn in other smaller parts of the branches if desired (fig. 5).

6. When you are finished, tie off the yarn end so your weaving doesn't unravel. Now weave in your nature additions (fig. 6).

Meet the Artist: Andy Goldsworthy

Andy Goldsworthy is an environmental artist. He uses materials such as ice, pinecones, rocks, flowers, and other nature items to build his sculptures. He is featured in a wonderful movie about his work called *Rivers and Tides*.

Installation at the Yorkshire Sculpture Park by Andy Goldsworthy

LAB 51 Sand & Glue Paintings

 Materials

- cover stock
- oil pastels
- clear glue
- sand
- cotton batting
- pencil

Tip

This is a fun process for the younger child—just use the largest oil pastels you can find for tiny hands!

Go Further

Try mixing some sand into acrylic paint to make a textural paint. Make only a small amount at a time because the paint dries quickly.

Think First: Sometimes artists add things to their paint or on top of their paint for more texture. Sand is one of those things. For this Lab, we are going to use richly colored oil pastels, and we will add sand for texture in places where sand might actually appear. The artist who inspired this lesson is Tim Wirth. His paintings are often quite gritty in texture.

Let's Go!

Fig. 1: *Begin the drawing.*

Fig. 2: *Add the glue.*

Fig. 3: *Sprinkle the sand.*

Fig. 4: *Add some cotton batting.*

1. Begin with either a light pencil drawing or jump right in with the pastels (fig. 1).
2. Continue to use the oil pastels until all the white paper is covered.
3. Choose the areas where you would like to add sand. In the example, our student made a beach, but you could make a desert, a path in the woods, the bottom of the sea, or even a giant hourglass! Use the glue to make lines or shapes where you want the sand to stick (fig. 3).

4. Take a small handful of sand and sprinkle it over the glue a little at a time (fig. 4).
5. In our example, there is a blue sky and puffy clouds. The student decided to add texture in the clouds with glue and cotton batting (fig. 5). What else could you add to your art?

Meet the Artist: Tim Wirth

Wirth recently stated about his work, "I like things like rock piles, cars stored in corncribs, and dogs running in ditches. I like the imagery of those things, but I also like the attitude of those things. Sometimes I like the attitude better than I like the picture. Sometimes I just like the picture." Wirth grew up on a farm in rural Iowa. He began studying art at Buena Vista University in Storm Lake, Iowa, and then continued at the Savannah College of Art and Design in Savannah, Georgia, where he received his MFA in painting. Learn more at www.timwirth.com.

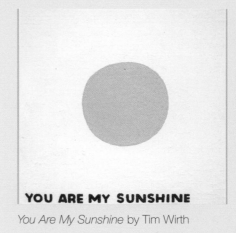

YOU ARE MY SUNSHINE

You Are My Sunshine by Tim Wirth

Tape Shakers

- two small plastic containers
- dried beans or rice
- masking tape
- acrylic paint
- egg carton for paint
- wash water
- paint markers
- newspaper
- waxed paper

Think First: Making a musical instrument is always fun to do. This little shaker is perfect for little hands and can be played along with your favorite music. Shakers are used in many types of music all over the world. Check out your local library's books on world music to find some more shakers!

Tip

The very young child will need shorter tape pieces than the older child. All little kids love tape. An adult can help to cut it from the roll and stick it on the side of the table so they can use it easily.

Go Further

Try making different shaped shakers and use different things inside for the noisemakers!

Let's Go!

Fig. 1: *Fill the cup.*

Fig. 2: *Tape the cups together.*

Fig. 3: *Cover with tape.*

Fig. 4: *Paint the shaker.*

Fig. 5: *Add details.*

Artistic Inspiration: Rhythm Instruments

There are many types of shakers from all over the world. Some have been traced back 1,500 years! People like to make music with rhythm instruments. Some shakers are made from wood, some are made from gourds, and others from seed pods. All of them are used to make music!

African Maraca

1. Begin by putting the noise makers (rice or beans) into one of the cups (fig. 1).
2. Place the other cup upside down over the first cup. Tape the cups together around the middle with the masking tape (fig. 2).
3. Continue wrapping the cups with the tape to cover them completely (fig. 3).
4. Place the shaker on waxed paper so it doesn't stick, and then paint the shaker on all sides (fig. 4).
5. When dry, add details with your paint markers if desired (fig. 5).

Resources for Materials

Australia
Eckersley's Arts, Crafts, and Imagination
(store locations in New South Wales, Queensland, South Australia, and Victoria)
www.eckersleys.com.au

Canada
Curry's Art Store
Ontario, Canada
www.Currys.com
art and craft supplies

DeSerres
www.deserres.ca

Michaels
www.michaels.com

Opus Framing & Art Supplies
(Stores in Vancouver, Langley, Kelowna, and Victoria, B.C.)
www.opusframing.com

France
Graphigro
Paris, France
www.graphigro-paris11.fr
art supplies

Italy
Vertecchi
Rome, Italy
www.vertecchi.com
art and design supplies

New Zealand
Littlejohns Art & Graphic Supplies Ltd.
Wellington, New Zealand
Ph 04 385 2099
Fax 04 385 2090

United Kingdom
T N Lawrence & Son Ltd.
www.lawrence.co.uk

Creative Crafts
www.creativecrafts.co.uk

HobbyCraft Group Limited
www.hobbycraft.co.uk
art and craft supplies

United States
A. C. Moore
www.acmoore.com

Ampersand Art Supply
www.ampersandart.com

Dick Blick
www.dickblick.com

DecalPaper.com
www.decalpaper.com

Golden Artist Colors, Inc.
www.goldenpaints.com

Hobby Lobby
www.hobbylobby.com

Jo-Ann Fabric and Craft Stores
www.joann.com

Michaels
www.michaels.com

Daniel Smith
www.danielsmith.com

Utrecht
www.utrechtart.com

Contributing Artists

Judith Andrews
www.judithandrews.squarespace.com

Darryl Joel Berger
www.darryljoelberger.tumblr.com.

Erik Boettcher
www.artstreamstudios.com/shop

Megan Bogonovich
www.meganbogonovich.com

Jan Burgwinkle
www.bemused.typepad.com

Lindy Carroll
www.lindycarroll.com

Judith Heller Cassell
Rochester, NH

Jennifer Curwood Stevens
Northwood, NH

John Terry Downs
Rumney, NH

Cada Driscoll
www.cadacreates.blogspot.com

Penelope Dullaghan
www.penelopedullaghan.com

Edibeth Farrington
Laconia, NH

Ashley Goldberg
www.etsy.com/people/ashleyg

Andy Goldsworthy
http://en.wikipedia.org/wiki/
Andy_Goldsworthy

Jessica Greene
www.jessgreenestudio.com

Heather Smith Jones
www.heathersmithjones.com

Jane Kaufmann
www.janekaufmann.com

Francine Kontos
Frantic100@comcast.net

Chloe Larochelle
www.chloelarochelle.com

Mati Rose McDonough
www.matirose.com

Albina McPhail
www.albinamcphail.com

Adam Pearson
www.pearsonsculpture.com

Carol Roll
www.nostalgicfolkart.com

Mitchell Rosenzweig
www.mitchellrosenzweig.com

Anne O. Smith
Strafford, NH

Tim Wirth
www.timwirth.com

Matt Wyatt
www.rochestermfa.org

I would like to thank the wonderful littles—Ethan, Ava, Kendall, Teagan, Camarus, Cidarah, Sydney, Owen, Lucy, Miles, Pearson, and Landon. Their hard work and continuous smiles made this book a whole lot of fun to write! I would also like to thank their parents who brought them to the studio and made them all so sweet.

Acknowledgments

This book was truly written over the past twenty-two years. These were happy times spent experimenting with art methods and materials with my two daughters in our home studio and hundreds of little children in other creative settings. I am truly grateful for these enriching experiences.

To all of my artstream students in years past and for all the inspiration they have showered me with—a big thanks! To my mom for letting me make art whenever I wanted to. To John Terry Downs for instilling fearlessness in both my art and my teaching in the early years.

To my family who supports my wild ideas and often takes me on creative side trips with theirs. I love them with all my heart.

To Mary Ann and Betsy at Quarry who make "making books" a fun, professional, and extraordinary experience!

And to the love of my life, Rainer Schwake, a guy who can get any group of small children to smile.

Photo Credits

© B. Christopher / Alamy, 57 (right)

© Peter Horree / Alamy, 47 (bottom, right); 53 (bottom, right)

iStockphtoto.com, 139 (bottom, right)

Courtesy of *tabula rasa* graphic design, 79 (right)

Courtesy of Wikipedia, 55 (right); 69 (bottom); 70 (left); 75 (bottom); 103 (bottom, right); 105 (right); 112 (bottom); 135 (bottom, right)

© Bernie Epstein / Alamy, 107 (bottom, right)

About the Author

Photo: Chloe Larochelle

Susan Schwake is an artist, art educator, and curator. She actively exhibits her own work in galleries around the United States and Europe and sells her work online and in her own gallery, artstream. Susan has been part of juried public art exhibitions, creating large-scale, site-specific works.

Her passion for teaching and making art with others grew from a tiny seed of an idea in the fourth grade. Working in such diverse settings as schools, community centers, special needs nonprofits, summer camps, intergenerational facilities, libraries, and her own little art school, Susan has taught art to hundreds of people over the past twenty years.

She created a permanent exhibiton of children's art, involving more than 100 local children, that graces the walls of a new children's room in her local library in 1997, and updated it in 2007 on the tenth anniversary. In 2000, she directed a similar project with 400 people in an intergenerational setting for a new multi-agency facility, bringing the staff, families, and clients more closely together through the process of making art. She as enjoyed many residencies in public and private schools, with whole school projects, and in special needs groups and single classrooms.

In 2005, Susan began a blog called artesprit. Through the blog, she embraced writing and photographing her world, meeting many new artists and friends around the globe.

She co-owns and is the curator for artstream in Rochester, New Hampshire. She enjoys bringing compelling group shows of contemporary art to New Hampshire. She is happy to be working alongside her husband every day doing what she loves most.

Blog: www.artesprit.blogspot.com

Website: www.susanschwake.com

Gallery: www.artstreamstudios.com